From 0 to 1

FROM 0 TO 1

An Authoritative History of Modern Computing

Edited by
Atsushi Akera &
Frederik Nebeker

UNIVERSITY PRESS
2002

OXFORD
UNIVERSITY PRESS

Oxford   New York

Auckland   Bangkok   Buenos Aires   Cape Town   Chennai
Dar es Salaam   Delhi   Hong Kong   Istanbul   Karachi   Kolkata
Kuala Lumpur   Madrid   Melbourne   Mexico City   Mumbai   Nairobi
São Paulo   Shanghai   Singapore   Taipei   Tokyo   Toronto

and an associated company in Berlin

Library of Congress Cataloging-in-Publication Data
From 0 to 1: an authoritative history of modern computing /
edited by Atsushi Akera, Frederik Nebeker.
    p.   cm.
ISBN 0-19-514025-7
1. Computers.   2. Computer software.
I. Akera, Atsushi.   II. Nebeker, Frederik.
QA76.5 .C724 2002
004—dc21   2001034058

Chapter 3 is based on an essay commissioned by Harvard University Press for the
second edition of *A Computer Perspective: Background to the Computer Age* (Cambridge,
Mass.: Harvard University Press, 1990). Reprinted courtesy of The Eames Office,
Venice, Calif.

Chapter 8 is excerpted from Luanne Johnson, "A View from the Sixties: How the
Software Industry Began," *IEEE Annals of the History of Computing* 20/1 (1998): 36–42.
Reprinted with permission. © 1998, IEEE.

9 8 7 6 5 4 3 2 1

Printed in the United States of America
on acid-free paper

Acknowledgments

The preparation of this volume owes a great deal to the IEEE History Center at Rutgers University, both for the time of staff members and for various expenses. Its director, Michael Geselowitz, and its advisory group, the IEEE History Committee, are to be thanked. So too are research assistants Dina Lowy and Yutaka Ito, who located many of this volume's images, and the IEEE Life Member Committee, which supported the project financially. James Cortada provided invaluable guidance to the project, and he and Michael Williams helped considerably in locating illustrations as well.

Contents

II. Software

III. The Computer Industry

Contributors

Janet Abbate is a faculty research scholar at the University of Maryland and the author of *Inventing the Internet*. She is currently working on a history of women in computing.

Atsushi Akera is a lecturer in the Department of Science and Technology Studies at Rensselaer Polytechnic Institute. He is currently working on a book, *Calculating a Natural World: Scientists, Engineers and Computers in the United States, 1943–1968*.

Sue Barnes is Associate Chair of the Communication and Media Studies Department at Fordham University. She has just completed her first book, *Online Connections: Internet Interpersonal Relationships*, published by Hampton Press.

Martin Campbell-Kelly is a reader in computer science at the University of Warwick, England, where he specializes in the history of computing. His books include *ICL: A Business and Technical History* and, with William Aspray, *Computer: A History of the Information Machine*. He is currently writing a history of the software industry.

Paul Ceruzzi is Curator of Aerospace Electronics and Computing at the National Air and Space Museum, a part of the Smithsonian Institution, Washington, D.C. He recently published a one-volume survey of computing since 1945, *A History of Modern Computing* (MIT Press, 1998).

James W. Cortada is an executive at IBM Corporation. He is currently writing a book on the role of information in contemporary United States.

Michael N. Geselowitz is Director of the IEEE History Center at Rutgers University. At the Center, whose mission to preserve, research, and promote the history and social impact of electrical engineering and computing, he also directs Rutgers' Science, Technology, and Society Program. An anthropologist with an undergraduate background in engineering and a Ph.D. from Harvard University, he has written widely on the social relations of technology and is currently conducting research into the role of immigrant engineers in the United States in the years before World War II.

Luanne Johnson is President of The Software History Center (*www. softwarehistory.org*). She has served as President of the Information Technology Association of America and was the founder and CEO of Argonaut Information Systems, Inc.

John A. N. (JAN) Lee is a professor of computer science at Virginia Tech; he was the Editor-in-Chief of the *Annals of the History of Computing* for nine years, and he is Chair of IFIP Working Group 9.7 (History of Computing) and author of *Computer Pioneers* (IEEE Computer Society Press, 1995).

Henry Lowood is Curator for History of Science & Technology Collections in the Stanford University Libraries. He is currently working on "How They Got Game: History and Culture of Interactive Simulations and Video Games."

Michael S. Mahoney is a professor of history and history of science at Princeton University. He is currently completing a study of the formation of theoretical computer science, *The Structures of Computation.*

Frederik Nebeker is Senior Research Historian at the IEEE History Center at Rutgers University in New Jersey. He is the author of *Calculating the Weather: Meteorology in the 20th Century* (Academic Press, 1995) and several other books.

Arthur L. Norberg holds the ERA Land-Grant Chair in History of Technology in the University of Minnesota. Besides being a member of the faculties of the Program in History of Science and Technology and the Department of Computer Science, he is Director of the Charles Babbage Institute. He is a coauthor of *Transforming Computer Technology: Information Processing for the Pentagon, 1962–1986* (Johns Hopkins University Press, 1996).

Brian Randell is a professor of computing science at the University of Newcastle upon Tyne, where in 1971 he set up the project that initiated research into the possibility of software fault tolerance, and introduced the "recovery block" concept. He has since then been Principal Investigator on a succession of research projects in reliability and security, and is now leading European IST Research Projects on Malicious- and Accidental-Fault Tolerance for Internet Applications (MAFTIA) and on Dependable Systems-of-Systems (DSoS). He has published nearly 200 technical papers and reports, and is coauthor or editor of seven books.

Robert W. Seidel is a professor of the history of science in the History of Science and Technology Program at the University of Minnesota. He is the author of *Los Alamos and the Making of the Atomic Bomb* and coauthor of *Lawrence* and is at work on volume II of *A History of the Lawrence Berkeley Laboratory*.

Earl E. Swartzlander, Jr. holds the Schlumberger Centennial Chair in Engineering at the University of Texas at Austin. He is in the Electrical and Computer Engineering Department where he specializes in application specific processor design. He is a serious collector of calculators, slide rules, and books that relate to the history of computing.

Michael R. Williams is Professor Emeritus of Computer Science at the University of Calgary. He is currently teaching courses in the history of computation and working on a large research project detailing the history of computing instruments from the 15th to 20th centuries.

From 0 to 1

Introduction

Atsushi Akera & Frederik Nebeker

Few technologies have had the impact of the modern computer. From the largest supercomputers used to design the hydrogen bomb, to the tiny microprocessor embedded in a bread machine, computers have become a ubiquitous presence in our society. Many scholars compare the computer revolution to the industrial revolution. Like the steam engine, the computer has transformed all aspects of work and leisure. On the other hand, there are those who continue to puzzle over the so-called productivity paradox. Despite the fact that the United States now spends close to a trillion dollars a year— nearly half the nation's total capital expenditure—on computers, software, and other information technologies, there has been no noticeable increase in the nation's rate of productivity growth. But whatever the economic limits of its impact, the computer has become an integral part of our culture. Word processors, automated teller machines, and computerized turnstiles mark the daily rhythms of our life. More fanciful developments in cybernetics and artificial intelligence, meanwhile, has left the chief scientist and cofounder of Sun Microsystems, Bill Joy, wondering, "Why the future doesn't need us."

For many, one of the most important historical aspects of the electronic computer has been its ability to continually renew itself. The room-sized mainframe computers of IBM generated as much enthusiasm in the 1950s as the dot-com phenomenon does today. The nation prided itself for going "online" with the first remote timesharing systems of the mid 1960s. *Time* magazine celebrated the birth of the personal computer, designating it man of the year in 1982. Few technologies have enjoyed such a long period of continuous innovation. The computer is therefore an interesting case study for technologists and businessmen alike who wish to explore why this technology has been able to remain so current.

Part of the answer lies in the fact that the computer, like the steam engine or electricity before it, became part of the technological infrastructure for a larger industrial economy. The computer has long since ceased to be valuable for its sheer computing power. What draws investors, entrepreneurs, and corporations alike to the computer is its ability to be a part of medical imaging systems, night vision scopes, DNA sequencing tools, and countless other devices. With the invention of the first general-purpose electronic computer, the computer was, by definition, slated to be used in a vast array of applications that had any use for computing or information processing. Much of the history of computing within the past five decades has been about tailoring the computer to new and different applications, as the size, speed, and cost of computing technology changed to open new possibilities.

On the other hand, this history is very difficult to tell precisely because of the diverse uses of computing. While some historians have written about the personal computer, others have written about software, or the early mainframe machines. The scholarship was also divided along the lines of those who have studied the military, commercial, and scientific uses of computers. This volume represents one of the first attempts to offer some historical synthesis by covering the full breadth of the computer's uses and development. All of the chapters are written by leading authorities in the history of computing. These authors have been asked to contribute a piece in their area of specialty. The volume is divided into three parts. The first and second deal with computer hardware and software, respectively, and the third takes a more focused look at the origins of the modern computer industry. Interspersed between these three sections are photo essays that offer a pictorial history of several different aspects in the history of computing. The contributors have also coordinated their work through meetings and discussions sponsored by the IEEE History Center located at Rutgers University.

Several important themes emerge from this volume. The first has to do with the complex, interdisciplinary origins of computing. Computers did not emerge through the isolated efforts of electronic engineers, but through a multiplicity of developments in physics, mathematics, communications, accounting, and an assortment of other fields. Even from the outset, the early commercial success of the electronic computer was built upon the foundation of existing applications. Scientific calculation and business data processing proceeded on mechanical adding machines, accounting machines, and tabulating machines. The skills of the operators and technicians who used these earlier tools contributed to the origins of the modern computer. Established manufacturers, such as IBM and Remington-Rand, also played an important role during the early development of the industry, through their organizational know-how and manufacturing and marketing skills.

Second, many of the authors make it clear that the rapid development of computer technology depended upon the fundamental pluralism of Cold War research. Unlike the television and automobiles, or nuclear warheads to cite another extreme, the computer developed through a productive tension between diverse military, commercial, and academic interests in the new technology. Computer timesharing systems, for instance, first flourished within an academic environment where resource constraints and the pedagogical interests made interactive programming a particularly attractive technology. But these systems then went on to succeed in the commercial sector. Likewise, the digital packet-switching technology of the Internet was first viewed as an experimental form of hardened military communications that also enabled military-affiliated research laboratories to share expensive computing resources. The Internet and other high-bandwidth digital media now promise to thoroughly restructure commercial telecommunications. Unlike the field of physics, where academic and commercial interests seemed to grow farther apart during the Cold War, productive exchanges continued to occur among different aspects of computing R&D. In fact, there was precisely a pattern of similarity and difference among the various uses of computing that made the computer a technology that was conducive to successive waves of innovation.

Finally, the computer industry does not appear to be fundamentally different from other technology-based industries from the standpoint of business strategy. The entrepreneurial and follow-on strategies of computer firms were similar to those of other industries. Even the network effect that has been used to describe the success of Silicon Valley follows well-known patterns in business history. For instance, the network effect, which encourages regional agglomeration, was also an important feature of the American machine tool industry. In fact, this shared effect goes back to the fact that both computers and machine tools became a technological infrastructure to a larger industrial economy. Given the successive waves of innovation, entrepreneurship has been a persistent feature of the computer industry. The continued presence of established firms like IBM and Microsoft has accelerated the pace with which new innovations are brought to maturity. As a consequence, barriers to entry have often risen quite rapidly in computing, driving the rapid progression from startup to shakeout that has occurred at numerous points in the history of the industry.

The individual chapters in this volume provide a depth of detail that cannot be captured in any short summary. Two of the three works that appear in part I of this volume deal with the prehistory of computer technology. Michael Williams describes how new developments in physics, applied mathematics, and telecommunications generated a demand for ever faster computing speeds. James Cortada, meanwhile, describes how familiar tasks in commerce, such as inventory and payroll, generated massive volumes of data that had to be managed by U.S. corporations. Cortada lays out the technical, institutional, and managerial antecedents of office equipment manufacturers that contributed to the postwar computer industry. Office equipment manufacturers, including IBM, were the most successful firms during the early years of the electronic computer. Brian Randell offers a decade by decade survey of major electronic computing developments in chapter 3.

Computers can do very little without software. In fact, the very notion of a general purpose computer required that each and every machine be programmed to serve the needs of specific users. Unfortunately, an acute shortage of programmers began to appear by the late 1950s as businesses and other institutions began to install a large number of computer systems. Computing was not yet an academic discipline, so formally trained programmers were few and far between. As described by historian Michael Mahoney in part II, the early technical work on assemblers, compilers, and other high-level languages was an attempt to deal with this significant labor shortage. By getting the computer "to program itself," it was possible to eliminate the more tedious aspects of programming work. Doing so, however, changed the nature of computer programming and the skills associated with this work.

Centralizing the computer programming work through a software industry that sold prepackaged software was another way of dealing with chronic labor shortages. However, as Luanne Johnson describes in her chapter, the software industry had a fitful start. The academic origins of computing, and the manufacturers' tendency to bundle their computer programs with their hardware, produced an impression that computer programs were a public good rather than a commercial commodity. Yet although packaged software remained a small and specialized business during the mainframe era, several contract software firms did successfully market certain products by the early 1960s. The fervent growth of the software industry accompanied the first personal computers. Because of their sheer numbers, economics dictated that operating systems and application software could be written and sold by specialized firms. Both a cause and effect, a large numbers of enthusiasts and neophytes began to use the personal computers for their pleasure and daily work. Paul Ceruzzi describes the origins of PC software in chapter 9. Meanwhile, the popularity of the PC helped to transform the Internet into a communications medium. In chapter 10, Janet Abbate describes the history of the Internet from its military origins as the ARPANET to its transformation into the World Wide Web.

Several chapters in this volume are designed to provide a different point of entry into the history of computing through the use of photographs. Visual images of the early artifacts in computing have become an important part of how we view computer technology. A close look the artifacts may reveal things about the technical, engineering, and manufacturing aspects of a computer that might otherwise escape written description. In chapter 4, Earl Swartzlander provides the reader with a narrative history of early calculating machines. In chapter 5, Atsushi Akera offers a visual tour of the early electronic computers. In chapter 6, J. A. N. Lee describes some of the early computer pioneers. The two chapters that appear after those on software (chapters 7–10) provide a different perspective. Susan Barnes provides a history of user interfaces. The mouse and pointer, for instance, which has become an essential tool for working with computers, had a quite early origin. Meanwhile, Frederik Nebeker provides a broad look at the different settings in which people use computers.

Again, part III offers a closer look at the origins of the computer industry. Arthur Norberg describes the early efforts of three computer firms, the Eckert-Mauchly Computer Corporation, Engineering Research Associates, and IBM. He provides a careful study of the technical challenges and business decisions that two entrepreneurial firms and one established office-equipment manufacturer faced during the early years of the computer's development. Martin Campbell-Kelly provides a broader picture of the early computer industry. By drawing on specific concepts found in other case studies in business history, Campbell-Kelly sketches out the tactics and concerns that firms faced during three different stages of the computer industry. In the final chapter, Robert Seidel reveals the extent to which the federal government facilitated the rapid development of the U.S. computer industry. The U.S. Atomic Energy Commission, the National Science Foundation, and other federal organizations served both as customers and important sponsors for research and development. The diversity of interest even within the federal government did much to expand the U.S. computer industry's capabilities and to improve its underlying technologies.

Each chapter ends with a list of suggested reading for those with greater interest in a given topic. There is also a set of appendices at the end of this volume that refers the reader to a wealth of material in the history of computing. In addition to a bibliographic essay, we have asked several authors to write about historical archives and online sources, existing oral history collections, and the intriguing array of computer history museums that have sprung up in recent years. We hope that this book sparks an interest in the history of computing and the many subtleties that have accompanied the development of this complicated technology. We also hope the chapters provide some interesting reading.

I

Machines

Computing before the Computer

Michael Williams

T he history of calculation goes back about as far as anyone can imagine. From the earliest times people have had a need to do simple arithmetic when gathering food and other resources. Undoubtedly the first primitive considerations would have been "is this enough" rather than "how many," but once some concept of numbers had arisen it would have only been a matter of a short time before the need for arithmetic raised its ugly head. With it, people began to look for ways to avoid this type of work, if only to record the result of a calculation to avoid having to do the work all over again when the same problem arose in the future.

Likewise, the attempt to construct complex calculating devices is not only a modern phenomenon but stretches back into history several hundred, and sometimes several thousand, years. Many different kinds of calculating devices emerged to ease the burden of computing work. Chapter 4 presents a history of "small iron"—the calculating machines that were once so common on the desks of scientists and accountants. I will use this account to introduce the reader to the "big iron" machines— large mechanical and electromechanical devices that were used to tackle difficult calculations—that were created prior to the development of the modern computer. These were the larger, more complex devices that were first envisaged at the end of the 18th century and became a reality in the late 19th and 20th centuries.

The "Engines"

While a German military engineer named J. H. Müller made some suggestions for a machine around 1786, it appears that Charles Babbage (1791–1891) was the first to formulate practical ways to automatically control a calculation in the 1820s and 1830s. He actually proposed two different machines: one that would calculate mathematical tables via the method of differences, hence the name "difference engine," and one that would be of a much more general nature (in fact it would do all of the operations involved in what was then known as "analysis"), hence the name "analytical engine."

Both of these were based on mechanical constructions from gears and levers, but were by far the most complex devices that had ever been attempted—indeed it has been stated that Babbage's drawings were only exceeded in complexity when huge battleships were constructed prior to World War I. Babbage never did produce anything except small working models of his machines, but he did inspire others to create a working version of the difference engine. In fact many individuals produced some version of his difference engine, even during Babbage's lifetime, and they were used to calculate various forms of tables until well into the 20th century. It is not surprising that no one at the time managed to build an analytical engine. It was not until about 100 years later, and only after considerable effort, that anything resembling the analytical engine came into being.

The difference engine was designed to perform the type of calculations that were necessary to create mathematical tables of polynomial functions—functions involving squares, cubes, and so on. While these calculations are not difficult, they are highly prone to errors because of the very repetitive and boring nature of the work. In fact all tables made prior to the general adoption of these machines were full of errors and had to be used with the utmost caution. In its simplest form, a difference engine consists of a number of "registers" (each consisting of many wheels that could be rotated to any of 10 different positions to represent one digit of a number), which were interconnected by adding mechanisms that would add the value contained in one register to another. The motive force was usually a large crank, which, when turned by the operator, would cause the appropriate additions to take place, thus producing another entry in the table. Babbage's plans called for an automatic printing device to be added that would automatically stamp the resulting number into a copper plate, which could be taken directly to the printers.

The first working difference engine—based roughly on Babbage's scheme—was produced by Georg and Edvard Scheutz, a father and son

Figure 1.1. The Scheutz difference engine (1853). The small wheels visible in the front of the machine could store a 15-digit number in each row of wheels. The mechanism at the top rear of the machine was the printing device. When being used by an experienced operator it could produce 120 tabular values each hour. Source: Science Museum/Science & Society Picture Library.

team working in Sweden, in 1853 (see figure 1.1). It won a gold medal at the Great Exhibition in Paris and was eventually purchased to form part of the founding instrumentation at the Dudley Observatory in Albany, New York. While it was of some limited use at the Dudley Observatory, it was several copies of this machine—one identical and several similar, but less complex—that introduced the scientific world to the benefits of automatically produced, and hence more accurate tables. The original Scheutz engine is now on exhibit at the National Museum of American History at the Smithsonian in Washington, D.C.

As mentioned above, Babbage actually designed a much more ambitious machine, the analytical engine. Although Babbage attempted to produce a difference engine, and only failed because of a number of practical difficulties—not the least of which was his overly ambitious plans—he never tried to build a working analytical engine. He limited himself to drawing up a set of plans. The analytical engine would have been roughly equivalent to the automatic calculating machines produced just prior to World War II, all of which required enormous financial and engineering resources to construct (see figure 1.2). Had he managed to find the resources, it would have filled a room the size of a small house and required the power of a steam engine to operate all its facilities. It was to be fed its instructions and data via punched cards (an idea he obtained from the famous Jacquard loom, see figure 1.3). Each operation card would be read, the operation executed, and then the next card would be read, and so on. He envisaged facilities for most of the operations that, today, are carried out on electronic computers. While never a reality, the

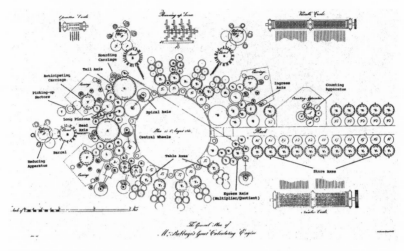

Figure 1.2. Babbage's analytical engine. This view from the top of the machine shows the major components. Each circle represents a column of gears and wheels that would have been 10 to 15 feet tall. The mass of equipment around the large circle was termed the "mill" and corresponds roughly to the central processing unit of a modern computer. The linear arrangement of wheels stretching out to the right, only part of which can be seen here, is the data storage facilities—which could be extended to contain over 100 numbers, each of 40 digits. Source: H. P. Babbage, *Babbage's Calculating Engines* (London: Spon, 1889).

Figure 1.3. Though a control device rather than a computer, the Jacquard loom was an influential precursor to the computer. Its method of storing information by the positions of holes in a punched card was copied by Charles Babbage in his plans for an analytical engine. Source: Science Museum /Science & Society Picture Library.

machine had a lot of publicity and it is known that some of the 20th century inventors of similar equipment were familiar with the device. It may well have been an inspiration for their efforts.

The Analog Iron

While Babbage certainly leads the list of inventors who proposed complex machines, there were many other mechanical calculators that proved to be much more effective in helping advance science and technology. These were usually based on analog methods of representing numbers (rather than the digital methods used by Babbage) where a value, say 2.7, would be represented by something like a gear shaft rotating 2.7 times or even a rod being moved 2.7 inches from its resting place. As these analog devices were capable of continuous movement, it was only natural that they be used for solving scientific problems that were of a continuous nature, such as problems involving differential equations and the integration of functions. Chief among these machines were the ones known as "differential analyzers" (not to be confused with "difference engines").

The differential analyzers grew out of a collection of more elementary machines that were usually used for simulating continuous activities such as the ebb and flow of tides (see figure 1.4). Lord Kelvin, in the late 1800s, devised a machine that would simulate the behavior of tides by summing up a large series of cosines. (It was known then that any complex waveform can be approximated by adding together a number of cosine functions of different periods and amplitudes.) His device would generate the individual cosine functions by moving a set of pulleys up and down at the correct frequency and amplitude. A wire joining all these pulleys together would, in effect, add all these movements together and the resulting complex waveform would be recorded on a chart mounted on a rotating drum. These tide predictors were in constant use around the world to predict tidal movements at various locations until about 1970.

It is really quite easy to set up an arrangement of pulleys like Kelvin's machine (or their equivalent in gears—the differential gear found on the rear axle of most cars is nothing more than a form of analog adding machine) to perform analog addition, subtraction and, with a little more equipment, multiplication and division. The major problem still to be solved with these machines was to provide some form of mechanical device to do an operation equivalent to the integration of a function (essentially finding the area under a curve). The ideas of Kelvin and others could not be realized as useful machines until a mechanical device known as a "torque amplifier" had been perfected.

Figure 1.4. Lord Kelvin's tide predictor. The dials could be adjusted so that the mechanism would generate the correct frequency and amplitude for each cosine that, when added together, produced a prediction for the tides. Turning the drive handle would cause the cosine generators to cycle and the sum, carried by the moving wire, would be recorded on the charts. Source: Science Museum/Science & Society Picture Library.

The methods of doing integration all rely on having a rotating surface (usually a disk like a phonograph record) with another wheel capable of moving across this disk and being turned itself by friction with the flat disk rotating underneath (see figure 1.5). The fact that there is almost no friction between the two wheels means that one cannot use the rotation of the secondary wheel to record its own movement on a counter or to drive further adding mechanisms—attaching anything to this wheel's shaft will simply cause it to slip rather than being turned by the large rotating disk. It was Vannevar Bush who first developed a torque amplifier (essentially a device to take the minute forces generated by the integrating mechanisms and amplify them so that they can, in turn, drive other arithmetical mechanisms) and incorporated it into a working differential analyzer that he produced at MIT during the 1930s (see figure 1.6). This machine was quickly copied in many different parts of the world and became a major source of calculation for the solution of continuous problems—mainly differential equation problems that were important to the design of new artillery used during World War II.

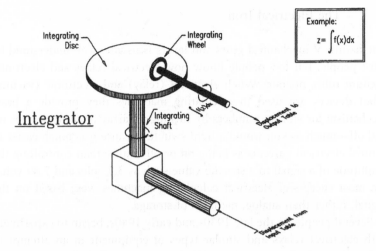

Figure 1.5. A disk–wheel integrator. The value of a function's variable, z, is fed into the mechanism by turning the lower shaft. This turns the integrating disk, which, in turn, causes the integrating wheel to rotate. The integrating wheel is moved back and forth over the rotating disk depending on the value of the function at the point z (i.e., $F(z)$). If the integrating wheel is near the center of the disk its axle shaft will rotate very little, if near the outer edge of the disk it will rotate much more—in essence the total rotation of the integrating wheel will be $F(z)\, dz$. Drawing by Mark D. Bowles, Ph.D.

Figure 1.6. Vannevar Bush examining his differential analyzer at MIT, circa 1933. The data was entered via the table seen behind Bush and was then transmitted to the various arithmetic and integrating devices via the rod and gear combinations seen in the main part of the photo. Output was usually in the form of graphs that were produced on tables similar to the input devices. Source: MIT Museum.

The Electrical Iron

The nature of mechanical gears and levers is usually well understood by most people, but few people know how electrical relays and electronic vacuum tubes operate. When electrical (relay) and electronic (vacuum tube) devices are used in calculating machines they provide a basic mechanism for storing numbers by turning an array of these devices on and off—much as you would a light switch. Because it is much easier to control electrical currents as being on or off (rather than controlling the amplitude of a signal to a specific value such as 3.5 volts and 7.89 volts) the most successful electrical calculating machines were based on the digital, rather than analog, methods of storage.

Several people, in the late 1930s and early 1940s, began to experiment with electrical relays and similar types of equipment in an attempt to construct a calculating machine. While we were still dealing with large-scale mechanical movements it was possible for a human being to keep pace with the movements of the machine and therefore control the progress of the calculation. The speed of relays (anything from a few to as many as 100 on/off movements per second) meant that humans could no longer control such a device. Therefore most relay-based machines resorted to the only form of automatic control then known—the punched paper tape that was in use both in telegraphy and automatic milling machines. This was essentially the form of control that Charles Babbage first proposed for his analytical engine about a hundred years earlier. The Z3, built by Konrad Zuse in Germany, was the first fully functional automatically controlled calculating machine. It was in use by December 1941, but was too limited to do much work except to provide a model upon which he could base more ambitious machines. This machine, like others produced by George Stibitz and Howard Aiken in the United States, was a product of World War II. Consequently, it was not really well known outside of military circles until well after the war was over. In the United States both Bell Laboratories and Harvard University/IBM eventually built electrical (usually relay-based) machines of much larger scope and ability. One of the first of these machines to become operational was the Harvard Mark I (sometimes called the Automatic Sequence Controlled Calculator) developed, in collaboration with IBM, by Howard Aiken of Harvard University (see figure 1.7).

Similar in many ways to Babbage's analytical engine, these machines were vast enterprises that required major resources to construct and operate. The Harvard Mark I, for example, contained 72 registers each capable of storing a 23-digit number, 60 constant registers

Figure 1.7. The Harvard Mark I was 51 feet long and 8 feet high. It contained over 750,000 components and used over 500 miles of wire to hook them all together. The control was via the paper tape reader seen at the right—the other three readers were for data—and output was via electric typewriters not seen in this photograph. Source: Division of Engineering and Applied Sciences, Harvard University.

set by switches, three paper tape readers used to hold input values (see figure 1.8), one 24-channel paper tape reader for holding the long loops of instructions, and electric typewriters for printing the results. This machine did a great deal of work producing ballistic and other tables. The speed of these machines was not great—usually no more than a couple of simple arithmetic operations per second. More complex operations such as raising a number to a power for finding a logarithm could take as much as a full minute. However, their ability to be controlled by long loops of operation codes punched on paper tape meant that they could be operated (sometimes unattended) 24 hours per day, and this was a dramatic increase in the calculation power that could be brought to solve complex problems. Aiken went on to develop three other machines, each of increasing speed and ability. These were used by the American military during the late 1940s and early 1950s.

After World War II, and despite the fact that electronics had already been shown to be a feasible technology for the construction of different types of calculating machines, several very large electromechanical machines were constructed and used by both the military and civilian scientists. Typical of these was the Bell Laboratories Mark 5, which was

Figure 1.8. The Harvard Mark I control tapes (containing the instructions that the machine would obey one at a time as they were read) were usually mounted on special devices behind the machine and then the tape loop was fed through holes to the readers on the other side. Source: Division of Engineering and Applied Sciences, Harvard University.

designed for military uses during the war but was not actually operational until 1946. The scope of this machine is impressive: it contained about 9,000 relays, weighed 10 tons, required 1,000 square feet of floor space, and was connected to 50 different pieces of teletype equipment. It had four problem input/output stations, each with 12 different paper tape readers, which could act in unison to control the operations of the machine. Each machine contained registers for 44 numbers. The machine could perform arithmetic operations in about one-third of a second (although it often took longer to read the operation from paper tape than to execute it). However, the day of the electromechanical calculating machine was drawing to a close and the use of electronics for calculating was to become the predominant technology.

The one "transition" machine between the electromechanical and fully electronic machines was the Selective Sequence Electronic Calculator

(SSEC; see figure 5.3) produced in 1948 by IBM. This machine was never considered as a commercial product by IBM but was produced to show off IBM's technological prowess and to be used as a high-speed calculator for certain high-priority scientific projects. It also provided a test bed for developing electronic circuits which would be used in later IBM products. The SSEC combined the best of high-speed electronic technology with IBM's expertise in electromechanical systems in that it used vacuum tubes where speed was essential (such as in the low-order digit positions of numerical registers) and relegated the much slower, and cheaper, relays to jobs where their speed would not slow down the machine too much.

Because of the use of high-speed vacuum tubes, the SSEC was capable of performing almost 250 elementary operations per second. This speed could not be kept up for long periods because the ultimate control mechanism was still the long loop of punched paper tape, which simply could not be read at these high rates of speed (see figure 1.9). The machine did have some very elementary facilities for storing simple short sequences of commonly used instructions (e.g., those used to calculate things like powers of numbers) and these could be executed at a high speed. Unlike the majority of the earlier machines, which were usually limited to executing one fixed sequence of instructions on a punched paper tape, the SSEC had 66 special paper tape readers, any one of which could be used to control the machine. Thus different sequences of calculation could be done by passing control from one tape reader to

Figure 1.9. Some of the special control paper tape readers from the SSEC. Courtesy of IBM Archives.

another, depending on the results computed so far. While not nearly as flexible as the modern stored-program computer, this facility did allow the machine to be much more useful than any of the early machines created in this paradigm. Two notable jobs performed on this machine were for the Atomic Energy Commission's design of the hydrogen bomb and a calculation of the position of five of the planets at 40-day intervals from 1653 to 2060. This latter job required the SSEC to do over five million multiplications and seven million additions and subtractions, which it did without error.

The Electronic Iron

Despite the fact that these relay-based machines were very useful and did a lot of computation, the real breakthrough came with the developments at the Moore School of Electrical Engineering in Philadelphia. Two rather junior employees, Pres Eckert and John Mauchly, suggested that electronics could be used to do calculations and thus avoid any mechanical movement which would slow down the process. Rather than doing a few operations per second, their Electronic Numerical Integrator And Computer (ENIAC; see figure 1.10) performed them at 5,000 operations per second. Because of the very pressing need for ballistic

Figure 1.10. Some of the main control units of the ENIAC (U.S. Army Photo).

table calculation during World War II, the proposal to build this machine was accepted by the military, and construction was begun in early 1943.

Before this time the vacuum tube had been used largely for manipulating analog signals in radio, telephony, and other related applications. Very little experience existed in its use as a digital switch. Even in large radio and radar installations, the vacuum tube proved to be an unreliable device. Big radar installations, which used about 200 tubes, gave significant maintenance problems. In comparison, the final ENIAC design called for almost 18,000 vacuum tubes. It was only the design genius of Pres Eckert that allowed the machine to become a working reality. ENIAC was doing useful work by the spring of 1945—too late to help with the war effort but it was soon put to work doing other military calculations.

While many people regard the ENIAC to be the first modern computer, there were significant limitations to the machine. Controlling the ENIAC was a major problem. Unlike the relay-based machines being built at the time, there was no possibility of feeding the ENIAC instructions on punched paper tape because it was physically impossible to read paper tape fast enough to supply 5,000 instructions a second. The solution was to control it by a massive system of plugs and wires—essentially you rewired the whole machine for each new problem, a process which could take anything from a few hours to a few days.

Still, the ENIAC represents a quantum leap in calculation. From a situation where automatic machinery could perform a few calculations per second we went to one in which a thousand times as much could be accomplished in the same time. The situation might be best grasped from the speculation, once made by the Head of the Moore School, that during its 11 years of useful life the ENIAC likely did more arithmetic than all of humanity had done from the beginnings of civilization until 1945!

Moreover, it was the all-electronic ENIAC project that gave rise to the modern idea of the stored-program computer. As soon as Eckert and Mauchly completed the design of the ENIAC, and before it was even operational, they realized that the complex plugboard control mechanism was going to limit the machine's usefulness. Together with other members of the ENIAC team they came up with the concept of having a much larger and more flexible memory that could store instructions (to be issued at high electronic speeds to control the machine) as well as the numerical information being used in the calculation. This "stored program" concept was given some exposure during a summer session course held at the Moore School in 1946, and several groups attending those lectures immediately began attempts at construction.

It was the stored-program computer that established a lineage of modern computers ranging from the first generation of machines built at universities, to the IBM 360 series, and then to the personal computer. And while this chapter was designed to survey precomputer technology, it could be added that many of the early stored-program computers also fell into the category of "big iron." As described in chapter 5, many of the machines, beginning with the limited prototype computer completed at the University of Manchester in 1948, also occupied entire rooms and laboratories. Still, these machines found new uses within an emerging movement to computerize society.

FOR FURTHER READING

William Aspray, ed., *Computing Before Computers* (Ames, Iowa: Iowa State University Press, 1990).

Michael Williams, *A History of Computing Technology,* second edition (Los Alamitos, Calif.: IEEE Computer Society Press, 1998).

Information Processing before the Computer, 1865–1950

James W. Cortada

The origins of the computer lie more in events in the United States than anywhere else in the world. Americans have a long history of acquiring information in many forms, such as newspapers and books in the 18th century, and either developing or adapting technologies to move it about. In the 19th century, for example, by the time of the American Civil War, this nation had an outstanding postal system and an extensive network of telegraph communications. Following the Civil War, developers of modern information-handling equipment rapidly appeared with a broad range of products. Most notable were typewriters, cash registers, adding machines, and, by the end of the 1880s, punched card equipment. (There were many other devices, which we will not discuss below, but which were made by the companies that concern us here. These machines included coin changers, check writers, and ticker tape printers.) Simultaneously, similar developments were underway in Europe but with less extensive deployment throughout its economy. To a large extent, the history of the development of the office appliance industry is really the story of how new technologies came to market and were used.

Focusing on developments in the United States illustrates the patterns of birth and evolution. It is a wonderful industry to study because it has been around for over a century. It is generally assumed that computers are of recent vintage and that almost overnight a whole industry emerged to sell and service this class of technology. However, nothing could be farther from the truth. While there were many sources of innovation that led to the development of the computer, the fact remains that by the time these machines had started to become a major fixture in the economies of the Western World, the key suppliers were primarily companies that had a long history of being in the office appliance industry. Burroughs originated in the 1880s, so did NCR. International Business Machines dates back to at least 1911, and if we count the Hollerith punched card business, back to the early 1890s. Unisys can trace its heritage back to at least the 1920s and if we count smaller companies that became part of Remington-Rand, then back to the 1890s. As will be demonstrated elsewhere in this book, the office appliance industry knew how to build and innovate precision equipment, had the resources to do it, understood how to apply such technology to information applications, and had the customers who eventually bought computers. Those facts alone would justify looking at the precomputer information processing industry. However, we do not even need the computer to provide justification because the office appliance industry was so large and so extensive by itself that even if the computer had never come along, we would have to acknowledge that the industry which came into being after the American Civil War was important. The same could be said of the office appliance industry in Europe by the 1910s. How did this industry appear so quickly and so widely?

As Michael Williams has demonstrated, there was a rich flowering of new technologies in the mid- to late-1800s that became the basis for thousands of products between the 1870s and the arrival of the commercial computer of the 1950s. Because technology in and of itself is not historically important until applied, the story of how information processing came to be is crucial to an understanding of the origins of the computer industry. Collectively as a nation, for example in the United States, the ability to develop, manufacture, and service complex technologies came from many sources over nearly a century. That portion of the nation's intellectual capital that could be applied to the development of mid-20th century computing technology originating in the office appliance industry included the firms that manufactured typewriters, cash registers, adding and calculating machinery, and punched card devices, such as tabulators.

There is a remarkable consistency in performance of the office appliance industry in the period from about 1870 to 1950, which makes it possible to generalize about how it came to be and operated. It is a classic example of the basic thesis of such business historians as Alfred D. Chandler, Jr. and David A. Hounshell, and of such business analysts as Michael Porter and economists such as Nathan Rosenberg or David C. Mowery, that technology comes to market when a company invests sufficiently in the development, manufacture, and distribution of products in a large-enough economy to gain market share and to make the effort worthwhile. They have argued that for a high-tech industry to do well over a long period of time, it must have a high degree of concentration, something that occurred in the office appliance industry. Historians of technology and business have also noted that a common characteristic is a period of chaos, one in which a rich variety of products and innovative technology platforms exist until standards are established. Products that existed before standards often emerged from the technologies and devices of those companies that did the best job in gaining market share and high sales volumes, not necessarily because of superior technology. The office appliance industry demonstrates this pattern at work.

But first there is the issue of definitions. Those companies that sold devices such as cash registers and adding machines between the late 19th century and the mid-1950s referred to themselves as members of the office appliance industry. Manufacturers of computers began, in the 1950s, to refer to themselves as members of the computer industry. By the end of the 1960s, they saw themselves as members of the electronic data processing (EDP) industry, the management information systems (MIS) industry in the 1970s or, simply, the data processing industry. Beginning in the late 1980s and throughout the 1990s, they spoke of themselves as members of the information technology (IT) industry. Economists, government agencies, and some historians have also added their own name to the computer era—the information processing industry—and some apply that moniker to the office appliance industry. To be historically correct, this chapter is about the office appliance industry, but to ensure that readers would understand that it was the precursor of the IT or computer industry, it was necessary to title the chapter "Information Processing Before the Computer."

Origins of the Industry

As mechanics, bank clerks, printers, and other tinkers began to develop equipment both in the United States and in Europe to meet needs that they perceived, the next immediate question to answer was how to manufacture and sell these devices. Looking at the events in the United States illustrates what happened. The key products of this industry were typewriters, cash registers, a wide variety of adding and calculating equipment, and tabulators and related subsystems.

The story of the typewriter is well known and so we only have to deal with several basic elements of its history. The first dramatically successful modern typewriter was developed by a printer in Milwaukee, Christopher Latham Sholes, in the late 1860s. He turned to a manufacturer of precision machines, E. Remington and Sons, and negotiated an agreement whereby they would manufacture the device in 1873. Fairbanks and Company, a manufacturer of scales, distributed and marketed the appliance. Over the next half century, Remington typewriters became widely used devices, with thousands of product innovations, and eventually many imitators. Between 1890 and 1920 the demand for these kinds of machines grew so quickly that over 100 companies manufactured typewriters around the world. Improvements in technology, lapses of patents or in spite of them, and a growing need for paper-based reports, all led to rapid development of the market. In the United States alone, by the turn of the century, over 100 firms operated, and sent nearly 40% of their production to markets around the world. As the national market in the United States grew, opportunity did too, leading to a major consolidation of the industry just before the start of World War I. As companies sought to increase their scale of production and their scope of distribution, they acquired regional firms. This effort resulted in a consolidation to less than a dozen major firms, including Remington, Smith, and Underwood. The major players then maintained their hold on the market essentially until after World War II.

Simultaneously beginning in the 1890s, as scale increased and technology improved, along with production processes, the cost of machines dropped so that by the end of World War I, typewriters had become the first office appliance to become a commodity. At the start of the industry, typewriters had been very expensive, costing approximately $100 in an age when you could buy a fine meal for 10 cents, and were sold by salesmen. By the time they had become commodities, customers around the world bought them from dealers. Improvements in functionality spurred competition and also a continuous round of price reductions. This pattern held true for manual, and later, electric typewriters. In fact, how typewriters became a subindustry of their own and were sold presaged what would happen with PCs in the 1980s and early- to mid-1990s. Many new models and basic designs appeared in the early years only to stabilize into some common patterns (e.g., same keyboard, typing with page facing typist) of design and use. The same came to be true with PCs, beginning with Osbornes, Apples, and IBMs, among many, only to end up with IBM, IBM-compatible, or Apple with operating systems overwhelmingly standardized on Microsoft.

What the typewriter experience did was to demonstrate how precision machine manufacturing had to be done to be profitable, what investments were required in order to sell products, and how, and to suggest what profits were possible. Because the typewriter became visible and widely available—over 100,000 were sold per year in the United States alone in the late 1890s—other manufacturers of office equipment could learn from the Remingtons and other vendors.

Cash registers came into their own and were also widely available in the same period as the typewriter. In fact, more people around the world saw mechanical cash registers than they did typewriters. Like typewriters, many vendors entered the cash register business in the first two decades of its existence but a few mighty winners emerged to dominate the market. Is there any reader who can think of NCR (National Cash Register) as anything but a major supplier of cash registers? James Ritty, a restaurant owner in Dayton, Ohio, saw the need for a device to control money at the retail level, and, with his brother John, worked on such a device in the 1870s. John H. Patterson bought one of their devices to help his retail coal business and then decided there was more money to be made selling registers and so bought controlling interests in the devices in 1884. He created the National Cash Register Company in Dayton and, over the next 15 years, despite many copycats and other competitors, came to dominate the cash register business in the United States and to become a major global supplier. To give a sense of the volumes, in 1918, NCR built and shipped about 1.7 million machines. This had become big business.

National Cash Register rented and later sold cash registers to retailers. Due to customer demands and competitive pressures, the cost of registers declined over the next several decades. Concurrently, new functions and innovations were introduced by NCR designers and engineers. Most of NCR's products were sold by salesmen, and many of the practices developed by Patterson became industry practices throughout the 20th century. For example, salesmen were trained how to use registers, were guaranteed their own territories, and had sales quotas—all features adopted by major vendors of computers, including Thomas Watson, Sr., creator of IBM, who had been a vice president of NCR at the turn of the century.

National Cash Register came to dominate the industry, although other vendors competed both in the United States and in Europe. In NCR's case, for example, in 1890 it rented just over 9,000 machines, but in 1896, that number climbed to over 100,000, and reached a million in 1911. By the start of World War II, one could not walk into a department store or even a small retail establishment without seeing a cash register and, more likely than not, one manufactured by NCR.

Its product development and manufacturing mimicked what was happening at Remington. Both patented every innovation they could, sued all rivals for patent infringement, and ruthlessly co-opted innovative ideas from competitors. Manufacturing stabilized into essentially the same process. In fact, Remington, NCR, Burroughs, and other major vendors began offering products in competition across the entire market that were built in the same factories. For example, NCR sold adding machines, although adding machines were the centerpiece of Burroughs' business. In the 1920s, IBM sold typewriters in direct competiton with Remington and Smith. Remington attempted to sell adding machines. Once national markets were established, and vendors realized that making an adding machine or a typewriter was nearly the same process, they began to broaden their product lines. What also encouraged them was the fact that many of their customers were also buying other classes of devices. Thus a department store that installed cash registers also needed typewriters and adding machines. This reality was not lost on any of the key vendors.

The world of adding machines and calculators represented yet a third facet of the office appliance industry of the late 19th century. They appeared at the same time as typewriters and cash registers, but unlike the two other machine types, calculators and adding machines added a whole new dimension to mechanical handling of information. They were more sophisticated in what they could do with data, for example, they could add and subtract and print the results. But, like the other devices, they were made essentially the same way, with a premium placed on manufacturing capability in precision machining and large volumes. They were sold to essentially the same class of customers. No organization of any size could do without them. Like the typewriter, they contributed mightily to defining what the office appliance industry was about. Many of the vendors who sold typewriters and cash registers also marketed this class of machine.

But they also had their own attraction. Accounting was a slow and laborious process before the adding machine or calculator. Later, more complex accounting practices became possible, such as cost accounting by the 1920s. More data could be captured and analyzed in a more timely fashion. This in turn made it possible to understand and control ever-larger organizations. Thus, for the same reasons that railroads, for example, rapidly adopted the telegraph, any sizeable organization acquired adding machines. Just like the other devices that had a long prehistory prior to some individual or organization finally making the technology widely available, so too the adding machine and calculator.

While many inventors were successfully at work in the 1870s and 1880s, the most dramatic cases are those of Frank S. Baldwin and

Willgodt T. Odhner, whose products were popular in Europe, and in the United States, William S. Burroughs, founder of the company that would, by the turn of the century be called the Burroughs Adding Machine Company. For a short time Burroughs had been a bank clerk and thus understood the need for such a device. He took on the manufacturing and sale of this equipment although not as successfully as his successors. But by the early 1900s, his was the most popular adding machine product line in the United States. Burroughs was to adding machines before World War II what NCR was to cash registers.

Like the other classes of devices, there were many competitors, which resulted in a continuous stream of product innovations from all suppliers and lowered costs over time. However, because functionality increased from the 1890s to the arrival of the computer, adding machines and calculators represented a much broader set of products than either typewriters or cash registers. In fact, between the 1890s and the 1950s, thousands of different variations of these machines existed, from simple adding devices to complex billing systems. The smaller, less expensive machines were sold just like typewriters, through retailers and retail outlets. For the most complex and expensive machines, Burroughs and its competitors had to use dedicated sales teams capable of teaching customers how to apply the equipment and how best to modify their accounting processes in order to exploit the technology. Vendors usually sold less expensive machines, while making large complex devices lease-only units. Customers liked this approach because the larger the device the more financial uncertainty and risk they had, thus leases represented a smaller commitment than purchase. Leasing also made it possible for vendors to swap out older devices with more advanced models (which were easier to manufacture and maintain) in response to changing market conditions and customer demands.

The market for these devices proved extraordinary. Burroughs illustrates what was happening. In 1900, Burroughs Corporation generated $323,000 in sales. Ten years later, revenues had climbed to over $15 million and doubled before the end of 1915. Like suppliers of cash registers and typewriters, it sold about a third of its volume in non-U.S. markets around the world. Key global competitors included the German Grimme, Natalis & Co. (better known as Brunsviga) and the U.S.-based Felt & Tarrant, manufacturer of the popular Comptometer. Several dozen vendors operated in Europe and in the United States by World War I.

The fourth root of the office appliance industry, and the one that was least connected to typewriters, calculators, or cash registers, grew out of the work of Herman Hollerith in the development of punched card tabulation. Hollerith's work is crucial to the origins of the computer because his devices manipulated data, created the commercial demand for machines that could operate faster and more effectively than his—later known as the computer—and which used his concept of the punched card as an early data entry strategy for feeding information into computers. His machines also needed to be built with precision, required constant innovation, and were adopted by very large data handling organizations such as railroads, insurance companies, government agencies, and major manufacturing firms. Often the same users of tabulating equipment also had adding machines, calculators, and typewriters, and cash registers if they had retail operations. Hollerith's claim to fame also rested on one other fact: his company became the centerpiece of what would eventually be known as IBM.

Hollerith developed his machines initially while working at the U.S. Bureau of the Census in the 1880s. In the 1890s he found customers who needed to analyze large bodies of data, like census takers around the world. He built and leased his own machines in Washington, D.C., and sold the now-famous punch cards to users. He had very few rivals in the early 20th century, which made it possible for him to expand the business. In 1911, his firm, known as the Tabulating Machine Company, in search of capital to expand production of machines that he leased to customers, and thus upon which he had to capitalize, merged with three other little companies to form a new firm called C-T-R. In 1914, Thomas Watson became general manager of the company and immediately began to focus on expanding the Hollerith part of the business. In 1924, Watson renamed the company the International Business Machines Corporation, or IBM. He applied many of the management practices he had learned at NCR, even brought product designers over from NCR to invent new Hollerith equipment at IBM, and eventually expanded his product line to include typewriters and some other office equipment. The major competitor for punched card services was the Powers Accounting Machine Company, which had approximately 5–10% of the market primarily in the United States, and in Europe, Machines Bull, which had an even smaller share.

By the start of World War I, all the key elements needed for an industry were in place: products, customers, applications of the technology, vendors, management practices, and a sense of identity. The primary customers for most of the products discussed in this chapter were office workers, and the largest market in the world was in the United States. The numbers tell the story. In 1900, managers and clerks made up 8.9% of the workforce; by 1940 that had climbed to 17%. Offices expanded dramatically. In 1899, about $50 million went into office equipment, in 1919, annual expenditures had reached $200 million, and, by the end of the 1920s, approached $500 million. By the end of the 1940s, that number neared $600 million. Even accounting for some inflation, the expansion was extraordinary.

Figure 2.1 graphically illustrates the growth of the office appliance industry. Four major lines of technology and products came closer and closer together over time, with many practices and manufacturing techniques being nearly identical. The same firms offered products from many categories of machines that at one time were independent of each other. To the right of figure 2.1 is a depiction in a circle of the major marketing activities of the industry. The more complicated a product the more customers relied on what is presented in the lower half of the circle. The smaller or easier to use a product became, the more this industry looked like what was in the top half of the circle. Once in place (by about 1920) the patterns depicted in figure 2.1 remained essentially intact until the arrival of the computer. Depressions and wars may have interrupted natural patterns of behavior, but did not slow sales. In the end, the pattern held as the deployment of such equipment expanded around the world.

Figure 2.2 plots the evolution of this industry on a classic innovation / growth curve. The figure illustrates that the office appliance industry is a typical example of what happens with a high-tech industry. It also demonstrates a pattern we would see again with every major line of base products in the computer industry (e.g., mainframes, minis, and later, personal computers, and which we are now seeing with PDAs).

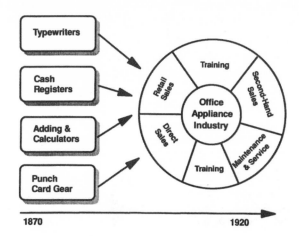

Figure 2.1. Evolution of U.S. office appliance industry structure, 1870–1920.

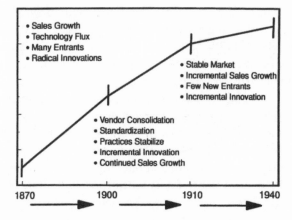

Figure 2.2. Evolution of office appliance technologies and sales.

So how many vendors participated in this industry? In the United States, for which we have excellent data, we can say that there were 26 major vendors of adding machines in the 1920s, 14 native suppliers of calculators, eight with the more complicated bookkeeping machines, and over a dozen suppliers of cash registers. There were two providers of punched card equipment. The major players across all product lines in pre-World War II America were Burroughs, Felt & Tarrant, Marchant, Dalton, Remington Typewriter, Underwood Typewriter, and IBM. At the end of the 1920s a dramatic event occurred with the first restructuring since the typewriter business merged into a few companies just before World War I: the formation of Remington-Rand, which included the typewriter business, other office equipment, and many paper supplies (e.g., notebooks, 3 × 5 cards, filing systems, and office furniture).

During the years from approximately 1890 to 1940, customers learned how to use a wide variety of equipment, finding applications for these. Accounting uses provided the major focus for tabulating, adding, calculating, and billing equipment. Americans used typewriters first in business and in government, then later in their private lives. Cash registers were, in effect, the first industry-specific application of information technology, made for use in the retail arena. In the 50 years before World War II, scientific and business applications expanded. New things became possible, like the U.S. Social Security Administration of the 1930s being able to collect millions of records and pay millions of Americans. Insurance companies could manage case loads on a national basis while railroads could control inventories of rolling stock and ship products across a nation that was over 3,000 miles in width. Photographs of offices in the 1920s and 1930s illustrate a great deal of information technology already in place: telephones, telegraphs, specialized wire services, typewriters, checkwriters, adding machines and calculators, even tabulators and card punch stations.

If you looked at the lines of products discussed in this chapter over their life of some 70 to 80 years, such as cash registers, adding machines, and tabulators, you would find that throughout the period vendors and customers worked together to produce thousands of innovations and models. Hardly a year went by without new product introductions or innovations from each product line. Catalogs from the 1910s through the 1940s grew in number of pages, describing additional features or whole new models of preexisting products. Companies that produced them also expanded. In 1928, the largest firm in the industry as ranked just by raw dollar sales was Remington-Rand with revenues of $59.6 million; NCR came in second with sales of $49 million, and in third was Burroughs at $32.1 million. Add in IBM and Underwood-Elliott-Fisher, and the top five firms in the industry generated revenues of over $180 million. In 1941, these same firms booked revenues in excess of $260 million.

From World War II to the Arrival of the Computer

World War II generated a vast demand for business machines around the world. Armies had to be paid, supplies moved around, and intelligence gathered. World War II led to the computer coming out of the laboratory and into practical use by governments in Europe and in the United States. There was an enormous increase in government and war-related use of equipment; but civilian applications never went away. While many machines were diverted from domestic use to government agencies, use proved so extensive that it would be difficult to imagine the war being fought without such equipment. For example, how could you plan a D-Day invasion of Europe on the scale launched by the Allies without using tabulating equipment from IBM? Or, for that matter, how could the Germans plan the extermination of millions of people without using information-handling equipment to analyze census records and keep track of their deadly mission? In every country involved in war, local vendors of office equipment were enlisted in the fight. The IBM plant in Germany supplied the German Army, IBM plants in the United States supplied the American Army. All major vendors became involved in complex research projects that exposed them to many new technologies (such as electronics) which, after the war, they began to apply to another whole round of product innovations. The result was that by the time computers had become viable commercial products, all the major office appliance firms had acquired the technical wherewithall to develop, manufacture, market, and service these machines.

Thus we are in no danger of underestimating the importance of World War II on the office appliance industry. If we look at base technologies and innovations, there were many. Using patent data as a surrogate measure of innovation, we see that six companies (Burroughs, IBM, NCR, Underwood, Remington-Rand, and Monroe Gardner) collectively received only 76 patents in 1940, but the following year 199, and 162 in 1942. For the rest of the war, the numbers were always 100 or more annually. Revenues tell a similar story of growth: in 1939, Burroughs enjoyed revenues of $28.5 million, in 1945 just over $32 million; in 1939, NCR had revenues of just over $37 million, in 1945, over $68 million; IBM booked $39.5 million in 1939 but in 1945 that had risen to $141.7 million; Remington-Rand experienced spectacular growth too, moving from net sales in 1939 of $43 million to $108 million in 1945. The implications are clear: with such growth, these companies had the assets and intellectual capital to enter the postwar period well equipped to supply new and existing products to a world that increasingly had come to rely on information and its technologies.

Conversion to a peace-time economy came quickly and the industry boomed globally. By 1948, in the United States alone, 100,000 workers drew paychecks in this industry. The industry remained essentially structured as before. Again, using the U.S. case, we see that the top five vendors at the end of the decade were familiar: IBM, NCR, Remington-Rand, Burroughs, and Underwood. They went to market with the types of channels of distribution as before the war: branch offices, dealers, and agencies. The larger the product the more likely it was sold through sales branch offices, the smaller the device the more inclined vendors were to distribute it through retail dealers and agents. One other very important point to keep in mind, particularly for the decade of the 1950s when the likes of IBM and Sperry-Rand began to introduce widely publicized computers, the lion's share of revenues for information processing products continued to come from such traditional sources as typewriters, cash registers, adding and calculating equipment, and punched card tabulators.

In addition to national growth in the United States, the traditional market for office equipment remained global just as it had been since the 1880s. The largest suppliers of office equipment were American firms, which routinely sold about a third of their products outside the United States. In Western Europe, indigenous firms sold primarily in local markets but always had a small presence in the United States. Using U.S. data suggests the growth in demand for traditional office appliances on the eve of the computer. Between 1953 and 1959, in the United States alone, foreign manufacturers of adding, calculating, and cash register machines quadrupled their sales, and they represented just a tiny fraction of the American market. In Western Europe the number of firms manufacturing and selling equipment kept growing back to pre-World War II levels. West Germany had 21 firms in the 1950s, Switzerland 11, Italy eight, and there were five major suppliers each in the United Kingdom, Sweden, and the Netherlands. The numbers are not as important as the fact that each major European country had multiple suppliers. In addition, they also had wholly owned U.S. subsidiaries. In Italy there were two, four in West Germany, five in Great Britain, and three each in the Netherlands and France.

Historians, economists, and business leaders measure industries by size of revenues. In the U.S., all office machine sales (including for devices we have not discussed, e.g., coin changers) in 1949 reached $764 million, but in 1951, $1.125 billion. In the latter year, IBM had 23.7% of the market, Remington-Rand 20.2%, and NCR, 18.8%. Burroughs played a distant fourth with 11.3%; all other vendors had single-digit shares but had been familiar to the market for decades (e.g., Royal, Underwood, Smith-Corona, Felt & Tarrant).

Summary

What finally happened to the office appliance industry after the arrival of the computer? For one thing, it did not disappear: IBM continued to invest in innovation of tabulating technology until the end of the 1950s, only getting out of that business in the early 1960s. It kept much of the peripheral technology (e.g., punched card input/output equipment such as printers) linked to computer systems until the 1980s. The Monroe Calculator continued to be sold until the 1980s when chip-based adding devices from Texas Instruments and Hewlett-Packard, among others, finally displaced the old mechanical adding equipment. Typewriters, and later, point-of-sale terminals, which performed similar functions up to the present day, were sold by NCR and IBM. Typewriters were also sold by Remington, Smith-Corona, and many other vendors until personal computers finally displaced most of the demand by the end of the 1980s.

With the arrival of the computer, however, fundamental restructuring of the industry began in the late 1950s and continued into the 1960s. The old Remington-Rand company underwent various transformations and mergers as it acquired computer manufacturing capabilities, and eventually became Sperry-Rand. Finally, from the 1950s to the 1970s, Unisys, Felt & Tarrant, Victor, and most of the typewriter firms were either subsumed into other organizations or simply folded. Manufacturers of electronics and other high-tech devices that entered the computer industry, such as RCA, Honeywell, and GE, eventually retired from the computer business, leaving the lion's share of the market to companies with an office appliance heritage or new firms that had not existed prior to the arrival of the computer. This pattern was true both in Western Europe and in the United States. The one major exception occurred in Japan, where electronic firms were able to retain successful control over its indigenous computer industry. But even some of these had earlier experience in the office appliance industry.

We have portrayed this industry as predominantly American. But it was also a global one from its earliest days. The archives of NCR are filled with photographs of people using cash registers in the most obscure corners of the world dating from the late 1880s forward. Burroughs collected similar photographs of its devices. User's manuals for IBM tabulating machines were published in over a dozen languages by the end of the 1920s. German calculators it seemed were everywhere, while the British kept introducing new products at every major industrial trade show from the 1880s forward. While American technology and vendors were large driving forces in this industry, they were not alone, although the majority of technological innovations originated in the United States.

This was also an industry that illustrated the value of scale and scope. As the great American business historian Alfred D. Chandler, Jr. had observed about so many industries, the office appliance industry required national and international markets in order to build the volume of products required to maximize efficiencies of manufacture and sales. Furthermore, it was an optimistic industry. Watson at IBM commented in the mid-1920s that less than 5% of all the Western World's accounting data ran through accounting machines. He told his salesmen to go after the other 95%! He was right. An influential student of American information handling—James R. Beniger—has noted that, as companies and government agencies grew in size, they needed to control their operations by using tools to distribute and manage information. That requirement motivated not only the initial inventors, such as Ritty and Hollerith, but also the companies that emerged out of their inventions.

This industry has left a heritage. Perhaps its most enduring aspect has been a large body of business practices and experiences which continue to influence the modern IT world. How sales people are paid, trained, and managed has not changed essentially since the 1890s. You can find lease agreements in the IBM archive dating from the end of the 1970s with the same language as appeared in Hollerith contracts of the early 1900s. Personal computers are sold today exactly the same way, with the same arrangements between manufacturer and dealer, as had existed first with typewriter manufacturers and then, with suppliers of adding machines, like Burroughs. Many manufacturing practices perdured for decades right down into the 1980s and early 1990s. These included how technology transfer occurs in large corporations across divisions, how laboratories are asked to participate in product development, and in the role the U.S. government plays in funding high-risk, leading-edge IT developments, whether in the 1940s or the 1990s.

This is not to say that nothing is new in the computer world. Far from it. The products today are very different and complex in their own rights; markets are approached through television advertising and Internet-based selling. And, of course, today we have software. Perhaps the most visible difference is how ubiquitous information technology has become. Going back to the U.S. case, by the mid-1990s, one-third of all American homes had a PC, and over 80% of all employees could not do their work without some reliance on computers, direct or indirect. Estimates placed the number of Internet users in the United States at over 5% of the public and with as many as 50 million users globally. More important, forecasts in the growth of use mimicked the growth rates of the old office appliance industry in the half century before World War II!

The office appliance industry grew in response to fundamental changes in how the economies of the world operated. As they increasingly adopted industrial capitalism as their economic model, and successfully developed the necessary structures to support this, such as corporations and to technologies, nations needed ways to handle large volumes of information. Just as many people had turned to machinery to make things and to transport products, so too one could argue that information would be subjected to the efficiencies of the machine. The office appliance industry emerged as part of this larger process.

FOR FURTHER READING

James R. Beniger, *The Control Revolution: Technological and Economic Origins of the Information Society* (Cambridge, Mass.: Harvard University Press, 1986).
Martin Campbell-Kelly and William Aspray, *Computer: A History of the Information Machine* (New York: Basic Books, 1996), Chapters 1 and 2.

James W. Cortada, *Before the Computer: IBM, NCR, Burroughs, and Remington Rand and the Industry They Created, 1865–1956* (Princeton, N.J.: Princeton University Press, 1993).

JoAnne Yates, *Control Through Communication: The Rise of System in American Management* (Baltimore, Md.: Johns Hopkins University Press, 1989).

The New Electronic Technology

Brian Randell

The successful completion of the first practical stored-program electronic computers (the Manchester University Mark I in June 1948 and Cambridge University's EDSAC in May 1949) marked the end of the beginning of the so-called "computer era." Although this was not apparent at the time, we can now see that most of the fundamental concepts of digital computing had appeared by 1950 and were embodied in the term "stored-program computer." Still, this did not mean that the technical work was done. In fact, few people foresaw the extent to which computer technology and its applications would develop—a process that continues to this day. This account is therefore about the successive decades during which many important advances were made to extend the usefulness and capabilities of the computer. These advances concerned both hardware and software: tremendous improvements in hardware speed and storage capacity coupled with great cost and size reductions enabled and motivated the development of a vast amount of highly innovative software, for a huge range of applications.

The 1950s

During the 1950s, digital computers moved beyond their early start as one-of-a-kind machines that were used by the scientists and engineers who built them. They became commercial products, manufactured in at least modest quantities by a growing number of computer manufacturers.

The first commercially manufactured computers were the Ferranti Mark 1, delivered to Manchester University in February 1951, and the UNIVAC I, delivered the next month to the U.S. Census Bureau. In the United States the UNIVAC had an initial market lead. However, IBM introduced its large scientific computer, the IBM 701, in late 1952, and the mass-produced IBM 650, or Magnetic Drum Calculator, a year later. It was not long before IBM overtook UNIVAC and became the dominant computer supplier in many countries.

Computers, though still very large and expensive, began to be put to a variety of commercial, industrial, military, and governmental uses by many different organizations. In the scientific arena, their use rapidly overtook that of analog computers and made possible far more extensive computations (such as the first numerical weather predictions) than had ever been feasible even with large batteries of desk calculators. In the commercial arena they became commonly employed as additions to, or replacements for, large punched-card tabulating installations used for major data-processing tasks (such as inventory control or payroll for a company).

At first, virtually all computer development was concentrated in the United States and, to a lesser extent, the United Kingdom. But during the 1950s other countries, most often in Europe, which had not already done so became involved in computer development and application. The total number of computer installations grew to approximately 6,000, and with the development of means of connecting multiple remote user terminals to computers, the first "online" systems were introduced. Perhaps the most notable was the SAGE air defense system. One of the most important advances was the invention of ferrite core memories, which quickly replaced earlier computer memories based on electrostatic storage tubes and delay lines (see figure 3.1). At about the same time, transistors, with their greatly reduced size and power consumption, came to replace vacuum tubes, thereby enabling the development of what became known as the second "generation" of computers, whose performance and reliability greatly exceeded that achieved by their predecessors. One of the first transistorized computers was the Japanese ETL Mark III, developed in 1956 by the government's Electrotechnical Laboratory; another was the Burroughs Atlas Guidance Computer, which was used in 1957 to control the launch of the Atlas missile.

The 1960s

The next decade saw computer centers set up in many medium- and large-scale scientific, government, and business establishments.

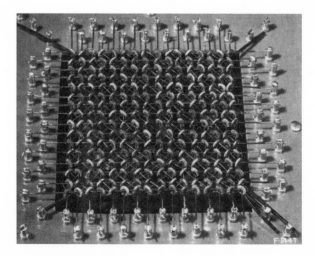

Figure 3.1. Ferrite core memory. Courtesy of MIT Corporation Archives.

Additionally, in the mid-1960s, the advent of the first commercial minicomputer, Digital Equipment Corporation's PDP-8, made it much easier to set up computers in laboratories, small businesses, and other environments. Prompted by these developments, and industry's consequential need for staff capable of successfully exploiting the new possibilities that computers were opening up, the first university computing science departments were created, usually as an offspring of mathematics or electronic engineering departments, and set about trying to justify their choice of title.

Computing and communications technologies started to come together. For example, the first online airline seat-reservation system, SABRE, was built by IBM for American Airlines. Also, AT&T introduced its first electronic switching system. The packet-switching principle, which involved breaking large messages up into sequences of small fixed-size digital "packets," which were sent independently and later reassembled into the correct sequence by the recipient, was developed at the Rand Corporation. The ARPANET project (ancestor to the Internet) to develop a resource sharing network, was launched by the U.S. Defense Department's Advanced Research Projects Agency (ARPA), and the first four computers in this network (at UCLA, UC Santa Barbara, SRI, and University of Utah) became operational in 1969.

Integrated circuits, albeit only at the level of SSI (Small Scale Integration), began to become available early in the 1960s, spurred in part by the needs of the U.S. aerospace industry. They largely replaced the use of discrete transistors, and integrated-circuit memory devices were challenging the dominance of ferrite core memories by the end of the decade. These circuits, since they were manufactured on a single tiny piece of silicon, enabled the development of computers that were vastly more powerful and reliable than their predecessors and that came to be called the third computer generation.

In those days, shifting to a new computer normally implied having to abandon or rewrite existing applications programs because of hardware incompatibilities. This situation led IBM in 1964 to introduce a range of compatible machines of varying power and capacity. This was the IBM System/360 series, which replaced their previously distinct line of mutually incompatible scientific and commercial computers. This strategy of having a range of compatible machines was soon followed by other manufacturers. Some even built System/360-compatible machines. As a result, software could be developed that would work on all members of a compatible range of computers. Given that software's "manufacturing" costs, that is, the costs of replicating and distributing copies of a software system once it has been developed, are extremely low, the resulting savings did much to spur the development of a software industry.

Memory capacities increased, and the first timesharing systems (which allowed a number of users to have simultaneous access to a computer) were brought into use, starting with CTSS (Compatible Time Sharing System) at MIT in 1963. Timesharing was largely motivated by a wish to improve the ability of the programmer and user to interact with the computer, though batch-processing systems (in which the computer executed submitted programs one at a time) remained the more common mode of operation. Increasingly ambitious applications and systems software projects were undertaken, and many organizations found themselves relying on larger and more complex computer systems than they had used in the past. Although there were some major success stories, there were also growing concerns about the cost of software and the frequent delays encountered in large software development projects. There were also repeated failures, some quite spectacular, in achieving performance and reliability goals, largely caused by the unexpected difficulty of designing, and in particular debugging, extremely complicated programs. The term "software crisis" was used by some to describe the situation, and "software engineering" was advanced as a hoped-for solution.

The 1970s

The early 1970s saw the introduction of the first microprocessors (silicon chips, each containing the entire circuitry of a computer processor;

see figure 3.2). The first was the Intel 4004, released in 1971, which came out of a project to develop a set of chips for an electronic calculator. The limited capabilities of the early microprocessors initially caused them to be treated as complex electronic components rather than real, programmable computers and to be regarded with more interest by electronic engineers than by computer scientists. Their use as the basis of a complete computer occurred first in the hobbyist market, starting with the Altair 8800 computer kit in 1975. Technological improvements soon led to the development of user-ready personal computers, such as the Apple II introduced in 1977. These machines were eminently practical. The next year Intel introduced a 16-bit processor, the 8086 (in which the word length was 16 rather than 8 bits, hence greatly enhancing its speed and capacity). A year later Motorola introduced the 68000, which became the basis for the Apple Macintosh.

The ARPANET and computer networking in general also developed rapidly during the 1970s. Other wide-area packet-switched networks were developed by various organizations in a number of countries. In 1974, IBM introduced the SNA communications protocols, and other computer manufacturers followed suit with their own networking architectures. In an attempt to counter this trend to proprietary network architectures, the International Standards Organization formally initiated work on Open Systems Interconnection (OSI) in 1977. It was some years before what came to be known as the Internet Protocol Suite swept the field, although the work on the basic Transmission Control Protocol (TCP) started as early as 1973.

Figure 3.2. Microprocessor. Courtesy of Intel Corporation.

Xerox's Palo Alto Research Center (Xerox PARC) also developed the Ethernet local-area network in connection with what turned out to be a very influential program of research on distributed systems, personal workstations, and human–computer interaction (see chapter 11). By 1973 they had developed an experimental personal computer called Alto that used a mouse and a graphical user interface. Ironically, it was not Xerox but other companies, including personal computer manufacturers, which a decade later exploited the results of this research most successfully.

The growing availability of online storage using large-capacity magnetic disks, and the consequent trend for organizations to use their computing centers as central data repositories, led to greatly increased use of database systems. These systems, the earliest of which dates back to the mid-1960s, provided a means for organizing and protecting data and facilitating its use by multiple application programs. The floppy disk was introduced as early as 1970 at the other end of the online storage spectrum.

The term "supercomputer" came into general use for an increasingly distinct, though evolving, category of computers. Such computers were significantly faster on large mathematical computations, for instance, for weather forecasting, and many other types of scientific calculation, than the most powerful standard mainframe computers. One of the most successful of these machines was the Cray-1, first announced in 1976. It was capable of doing over a hundred million arithmetic operations per second.

The 1980s

This decade saw the transformation of the ARPANET and other networks into the Internet, and the start of its explosive growth. Experiments with the TCP/IP protocol had begun in 1980, and the switchover to its use was completed by 1983. The 1.5 Mbps (million bits per second) National Science Foundation backbone was created in 1986, and by the end of the decade there were several hundred thousand hosts connected to the Internet. (These developments are more fully described in chapter 10.)

The 1980s also saw the personal computer market grow explosively. This was made possible by technological advances, but was fueled also by IBM's entry into the market in 1981, with their first Personal Computer (PC), based on the Intel 8086 microprocessor. Three years later, Apple introduced the Macintosh computer, with a graphical user interface embodying many ideas from Xerox PARC's research, ideas that Microsoft later made use of in their eventually dominant Windows operating system for the IBM PC.

The improved performance of personal computers, and growth of the personal computer market, were helped by, and contributed to, the increasing strength of the Japanese and other Far-Eastern manufacturers. Somewhat higher performance than that available from computers such as the PC and the Macintosh was provided by personal workstations, which were usually networked together and ran the UNIX operating system. However, the distinction between personal computers and personal workstations also began to disappear.

Toward the other end of the market, the decade saw the move towards the use of various forms of parallel processing (making it possible to execute multiple operations simultaneously) in order to gain increased performance over and above that provided by hardware improvements. Some of these were fairly conventional, while others were quite novel. An example of the latter was the Connection Machine, built in 1987, which contained 64,000 processors and required very different programming techniques. However, such technical developments were overshadowed by the commercial success of packaged software, produced almost entirely for the most popular types of personal computers. This new software included sophisticated general-purpose applications (word-processing, financial management, graphical design, etc.), as well as a vast range of computer games.

This led to the introduction of a myriad of specialist application packages intended for use by a great variety of organizations and individuals, many of whom regarded their computers not as general-purpose computers but as specialized tools used, for example, solely for preparing documents or for performing standard financial calculations. In addition, computers were embedded into all sorts of devices such as central-heating systems, dishwashers, and automobiles, where they were typically used unknowingly by the consumer. An analogy can be drawn with the electric motor. Originally, motors were very large and expensive and they were used to power complete factories. However, they were improved and miniaturized to the point where people have no idea how many electric motors they have in their own household. Likewise, people can no longer count how many digital computers they own.

Recognition of the economic and strategic importance of computing and communications led various countries to undertake major "information technology" initiatives. Japan in particular set up several major projects, including the so-called Fifth Generation Project. The term "fifth generation" was intended to dramatize the novelty not of the technology they would employ, as had been the case up through the third generation of computers, but of the architectures they hoped to develop. (There was no general consensus as to the characteristics of "fourth generation" computers at the time, although the term was later used to refer to certain types of programming languages.) The fifth generation architectures were to be specifically designed to perform logical inferencing rather than conventional computation, which would allow them to support advanced artificial intelligence applications. Various collaborative research and development programs that were subsequently launched in the United States and Europe, partly in response to the Fifth Generation Project, were mostly much more general in their aims and scope.

Concluding Remarks

In just 40 years a major new industry had come into existence, one that the world came to depend critically upon. This was an industry whose amazing growth rate showed, and still shows, little sign of diminishing. The principal factor for this growth had of course been the progress in electronic and microelectronics technologies, much of which were advanced through military support. Improvements to various storage technologies were also crucial. One measure of this still-continuing progress has been the ever-greater density of components, so helping both to increase speed and capacity while reducing the cost of computers.

Gordon Moore, a founder both of Fairchild Semiconductor Corporation and later of Intel, predicted in 1964 that the number of individual components on a chip would double every year, and this prediction, known as "Moore's law" has been roughly borne out over the decades since (see figure 3.3). This progress was a result of a variety of scientific investigations and engineering developments, which justified continued expenditures in these areas. Various improvements also tended to reinforce each other, leading to exponential growth in all sorts of measures such as memory size, processor speed, and storage access rate. These exponential growth rates have continued for many years, with dramatic effects. For example, semiconductor memory prices have declined by a factor of 10 every five years. Moreover, there is considerable unanimity among experts that these growth rates will continue for some years to come. They agree that fundamental technological limits are a long way from being reached.

Such technological progress has also accelerated the growth of the global information network. Meanwhile, the significance of networks

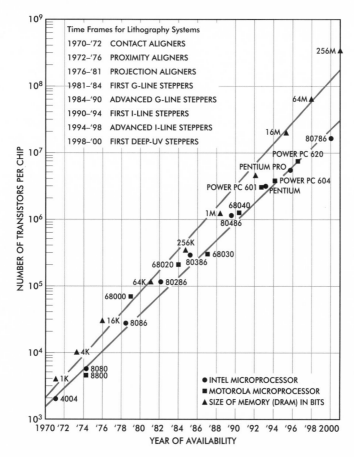

Figure 3.3. Moore's law. Chart by Lisa K. Braiman. Source: VLSI Research, Inc.; Integrated Circuit Engineering Corporation.

has been characterized by another law, one formulated by one of the developers of the Ethernet, Bob Metcalf, who has suggested that the importance of a network varies with the square of the number of the people that it interconnects—something which the success and impact of the Internet attests to very vividly.

Last, but by no means least, the vast proliferation of computers, and the emergence of numerous standards—either formal or ad hoc—has created a vast and varied market for software that enables the large costs involved in creating high-quality software to be successfully amortized over huge numbers of customers. This has led to the building of a tremendously important international software industry, producing not just general purpose software such as operating systems, but also an immense variety of applications software, as well as software for an incredible variety of systems and devices that contain embedded computers.

ACKNOWLEDGMENTS

A number of colleagues have greatly helped to improve both the form and the content of this account by constructively criticizing early drafts. In particular, I would like to acknowledge the assistance I have received from Tom Anderson, Bernard Cohen, Martin Campbell-Kelly, Jim Horning, Pete Lee, Maurice Wilkes, and Mike Williams. This summary of and commentary on developments in computing over the period 1950 to 1990 is based on one that was commissioned by Harvard University Press for the second edition of *A Computer Perspective: Background to the Computer Age* (Cambridge, Mass.: Harvard University Press, 1990). Reprinted courtesy of The Eames Office, Venice, Calif.

FOR FURTHER READING

M. Campbell-Kelly and W. Aspray, *Computer: A History of the Information Machine* (New York: Basic Books, 1996).

C. Eames and R. Eames, *A Computer Perspective: Background to the Computer Age,* new edition (Cambridge: Harvard University Press, 1990).

M. R. Williams, *A History of Computer Technology* (Englewood Cliffs, N.J.: Prentice-Hall, 1985).

4

Calculating Machines

Earl E. Swartzlander, Jr.

The various aids to calculation have a long history in the history of humanity. Early forms of the abacus were used in the Middle East by the early Greek times, and the modern wire-and-bead abacus was used in China by the 12th century (see figure 4.1). However, it was during the 17th century that Western Europeans began to explore new ways of devising mechanical aids to calculation. In part, the development owed its origins to the improved metalworking capabilities of European countries. The manufacture of clocks, ornaments, and scientific instruments made it easier to design the earliest calculators and to have someone fabricate their delicate components. At the same time, the earliest calculators were a product of the cultural and intellectual developments of Europe. Oceanic exploration, the rise of new centers of learning, and most importantly, advances in mathematics gave rise to a new interest in numbers and calculation. This chapter offers a brief look at the various calculating instruments that have been used since this time.

Manual Adders

While subsequent devices were designed to perform a range of arithmetic operations, early devices were designed only to add, and usually, to subtract. All of the earliest adders were hand operated. The earliest of these were activated by a stylus, which is a wooden stick similar in size to a pencil. As with the adder that Blaise Pascal had built in 1642 (see figure 4.2), a person used a stylus to turn the wheels corresponding to each of the digits of a number, which advanced the value depicted in the results register. Jean Lepine was one of the other inventors who built an early stylus-driven adder.

The very simplicity of these devices, along with the general rise in numeracy (a concept similar to literacy, but applied to numbers and arithmetic), allowed stylus-activated adders to remain in common use until quite recent times. As small businesses and households began making increased use of calculation in their daily lives, the kinds of aids used by mathematicians and scientists in previous centuries became an object of convenience. Furthermore, advances in mass production made it possible to produce reliable stylus driven adders inexpensively and in large quantities. One such device was the "Calcumeter," which appeared shortly after 1900 (see figure 4.3). James J. Walsh invented

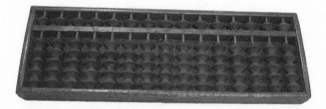

Figure 4.1. Although the abacus is often thought of as a Far Eastern device, it originated in the Middle East, from which it spread to both Europe and China. Despite its simplicity, a very experienced user could operate an abacus at a speed that rivaled that of electrically driven calculating machines.

Figure 4.2. Pascal's adder. Pascal, along with other contemporaries, designed and built stylus-driven adders during the 17th century. While these machines were instrumental in creating the general form of the mechanical arithmetic machine, they were often mere curiosities. Courtesy of IBM Archives.

Figure 4.3. James J. Walsh's Calcumeter. The adding mechanism had a leaf spring for each digit, which acted as a "detent." This was a way of storing energy in a spring to help perform a carry. This had a big advantage: going from 9,999.99 to 10,000.00 by adding one cent does not require a large amount of force from the stylus, since the required energy is already stored in the springs.

the Calcumeter, and held two patents for this device. As many as 100,000 units may have been produced before production ended some time before 1920.

It is possible that the Calcumeter declined because of price competition from the "Pangborn" and the "Lightening Calculator." Both of these devices were mass-produced adders. They were constructed from formed sheet metal, and hence they could be produced—and sold—at a very low price. These devices were never meant to be repaired. But whereas scientists and commercial businesses could purchase more reliable and specialized machines, casual users were adequately served by this simple device.

One of the difficulties with stylus-driven adders was the amount of force it took to propagate carries. For example, in going from 99,999 to 100,000, a one is added in the units position and five carries have to propagate. While this was not a problem for the occasional user, banks, utilities, and other companies whose staff tallied numbers many hours each day were vitally concerned with the ease of entering numbers. Between 1885 and 1886, Dorr E. Felt designed the popular Comptometer, which had a "key driven" action (see figure 4.4). The force of depressing a key advanced the wheels that displayed the sum. At about the same time (1886) William S. Burroughs developed a similar mechanism which can be described as the "crank-activated adder." While the Burroughs machines also had a keyboard, they did not execute the addition when the keys were depressed. Instead, the machine waited until the operator "pulled the crank." It was easier to press the keys with this design, and operators could visually inspect the numbers they were about to add or subtract before they pulled the crank. The extra force available in the Burroughs adding machines was frequently also used to operate a printer.

Figure 4.4. The Comptometer, shown here, was a "full keyboard" machine. This means that each digit position has keys numbered from 1 to 9. In a manner analogous to the stylus-driven adder, depressing a particular key advanced the corresponding digit of the results register an amount equal to the number represented by the key. Aside from superficial changes to the design of the case, the popular Comptometers changed little from 1880 to 1950.

This was the era of invention. The profits of business and their need for efficient operations gave rise to many other efforts to improve the adding machine. For example, many businesses needed to not only add numbers, but to print the results on a ledger that they kept as a part of their financial records. While the early Burroughs machines could print numbers, it did so at the back of the machine which made it hard to read. William H. Pike, a former employee of Burroughs, developed a "visible" printing adding machine that printed the results at the top of the mechanism, which made the figures instantly visible (see figure 4.5). This allowed Pike to form his own company.

The Early Calculators

While many users were adequately served by machines that could perform addition and subtraction, others were interested in machines that would also perform multiplication and division. Within the realm of

Figure 4.5. Burroughs produced a huge number of machines based on William H. Pike's design, first as "Pike" machines and then as Burroughs Class 3 machines, such as the example pictured here. Like the Comptometers the Burroughs machines were also "full keyboard" machines.

commerce, large businesses and mercantile houses purchased goods in such quantities, and paid taxes or assessed figures on these commodities in such a way that multiplying two numbers, such as the number of cases and a price, was a common chore. Likewise, statistical calculations, employed for the national census and in the actuarial calculations of the insurance industry, stood to benefit from machines that could aid an operator in performing division. The most demanding calculations occurred within the domain of science and engineering. Here, the mathematical equations used by physicists and specialized engineers mimicked the complexities of the phenomena they wished to model or understand. Multiplication and division was a common task for many who worked in technical fields.

Within this chapter, I reserve the term *calculators* to refer to machines that could not only add and subtract, but also perform multiplication and sometimes division. The earliest calculators were developed by Wilhelm Schickard in 1621 and Gottfried Leibniz in 1674 (see figure 4.6). The early

Figure 4.6. Leibniz's calculator. Leibniz designed the stepped wheel mechanism and used it to construct a calculator in 1694. Shifting the carriage facilitates multiplication via repeated additions and division via repeated subtractions. Courtesy of IBM Archives.

date of these calculators should not be surprising. Technically it is possible to perform a multiplication through a simple process of repeated addition. To multiply any number by a factor of 2 to 9, it is necessary merely to retain the number being added—just like in the early Burroughs machines—and add it that many times into the results register. Meanwhile, using a mechanism to shift the carriage from the units to the tens to the hundreds place, and so on, made it possible to multiply a number (the multiplicand) by a value greater than 10 (the multiplier).

Leibniz's stepped wheel served as the basis for many subsequent mechanical calculators. Unlike the stylus-driven adders, the stepped wheel mechanism provided a way to set the multiplicand, while a separate physical movement was used to carry out each step of the addition and multiplication. As with the adders, there were different possibilities for actuating the basic adding mechanism of a calculator. However, given the frequent use of repeated addition, a rotary crank that added a number into the results register once with each rotation proved to be a convenient form of manual operation (see figure 4.7). Despite the practical design of Leibniz's mechanism, the mechanical intricacies of a device with a shifting carriage made it difficult to produce reliable calculators until there were considerable advances in standardized parts and precision manufactures. Thomas de Colmar's Arithmometer was the first stepped wheel calculator to be produced in substantial quantities. Later machines, such as the Millionaire and TIM (Time Is Money) calculators were also based on the stepped wheel design.

Meanwhile, Frank S. Baldwin and Willgodt T. Odhner developed the *pin wheel* rotary crank-operated calculator between 1873 and 1878 (see figure 4.8). Baldwin developed the basic pin wheel mechanism, which provides the same basic function as the Leibniz stepped wheel

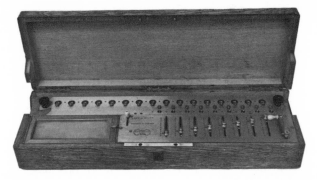

Figure 4.7. The Thomas de Colmar Arithmometer. The crank, located on the right, adds the number represented on the slide levers into the register mounted in the upper half of the machine. The register slides, which makes it possible to multiply two large numbers. Courtesy of Robert K. Otnes.

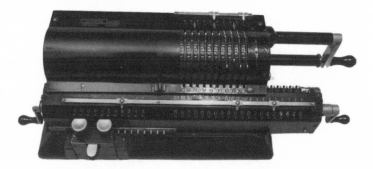

Figure 4.8. The Original Odhner. The extra register on the left-hand side of the carriage (here showing the number 8712) is useful for both multiplication and division. This register counts the number of rotations of the crank (at each position of the carriage) thereby providing a convenient reading of the multiplier or the quotient.

mechanism. Odhner then developed and incorporated a reliable carry mechanism. Odhner began producing his machines in Russia, but after the Russian Revolution he moved his production to Sweden, where he offered his machines under the name of Original Odhner.

Although the Odhner was similar in operation to the Arithmometer, the vertical arrangement of the pin wheels contributed to a more compact and rugged design. Apparently liberal patent licensing arrangements permitted many different companies to produce pin wheel calculators of similar design. The German Brunsviga and the American Marchant were quite similar to the Original Odhner depicted in figure 4.8.

Meanwhile, the early decades of this century brought electric motors to various kinds of office machinery. The increased feminization of the clerical work force made it attractive for employers and manufacturers alike to consider electrifying their office equipment. Whether or not gender made any difference in the operation of these devices, electric motors made it possible to reduce the physical labor associated with office machines, since they would respond readily to the touch of an operator. Electrification certainly improved the speed of typewriters, and typewriter manufacturers such as Underwood and Burroughs were among the first to employ electric motors in their equipment. The same firms placed motors in their adding and accounting machines. Other firms, including R. C. Allen, Allen-Whales, Sundstrand, and Victor also introduced extensive lines of electric adders.

Electric motors were also popular additions to calculators. Given the rotary motion that served as the basis for repeated addition, an electric motor provided a convenient means of carrying out this operation. Three brands were especially popular in the United States, namely the Friden, Marchant, and Monroe calculators. The more advanced machines built by these firms, such as the Marchant Figure-Matic shown in figure 4.9, had electrified carriages and performed single-digit multiplication by automatically turning the mechanism a prescribed number of rotations. Friden also offered a wide range of electric calculators that culminated in

Figure 4.9. The Marchant Figure-Matic. The earliest calculators built by Marchant were manual crank-operated calculators (similar to the Original Odhner). However, later Marchant machines like the electrified Figure-Matic depicted here, had full keyboards, which reflected their frequent use in accounting and clerical applications.

Figure 4.10. Among the most advanced mechanical desktop calculators were Friden's SRW and SRQ models. The Friden SRW is shown here. These were the only mechanical calculators that could automatically compute square roots.

the SRW model shown in figure 4.10, which could calculate the square root of a number automatically.

All of these machines—the Marchant, Monroe, and Friden—were highly sought after during World War II. They served as a basic tool for the accounting and logistics operations of the war, both by businesses and the military services. The Army and Navy's ordnance departments also used these calculators to produce artillery range tables for the new kinds of artillery they built during the war. In fact, these calculators were being used for just such a purpose at the Moore School of Electrical Engineering. However, the Moore School could not meet its production schedules for artillery tables using its electric calculators, thereby giving John Mauchly and Presper Eckert an opportunity to build an electronic device that was intended to meet the demands of war.

Electronic Calculators

Even the earliest electronic computers were a thousand, if not tens of thousands of times faster than electric calculators. However, early computers were also large, expensive machines. They occupied entire rooms, and the huge number of vacuum tubes made it necessary for a staff of trained technicians to constantly service these machines. Moreover, the high cost of electronic computers meant that a professional staff of as many as 30 to 50 people had to operate each machine to ensure their efficient use. This arrangement was not always compatible with the traditional work routines of scientists, engineers, and other potential users. In particular, the effort of having to submit a problem and then wait many hours for the results did not satisfy the researcher's need for immediate results. Certainly computers were essential to new kinds of scientific and engineering problems such as the development of the hydrogen bomb. On the other hand, many researchers continued to rely on more modest calculating machinery.

Still, there was an increased interest in high-speed calculation after World War II. The Cold War created a demand for new military technologies, and mathematical modeling and analysis became commonplace in fields such as aircraft engineering and guided missile design. International Business Machines was among the first to consider using vacuum tubes within a more modest line of electronic calculating equipment. The company demonstrated its IBM 603 Electronic Multiplier in 1946, and then introduced its more elaborate IBM 604 Electronic Calculating Punch two years later. A collaboration between IBM and one of Southern California's aircraft manufacturers, Northrop, led to IBM's Card Programmed Electronic Calculator. This was an even more versatile machine that had a limited electromechanical programming capability.

However, even the early electronic calculators built by IBM were elaborate machines that required a staff of specially trained operators. It remained the task of other firms to develop smaller electronic calculators. Early units were built by Anita and Wang with miniaturized vacuum tubes. Friden and Hewlett-Packard developed calculators which used transistors to drive a small cathode ray tube (CRT) display. All were desktop models that cost upwards of several thousand dollars. Nonetheless these units could be found beside a laboratory workbench or in a central *calculating room* within a larger research or engineering facility. In either case, both researchers and technicians could use these machines themselves to perform their calculations. Although these machines had primitive programming capabilities, the lack of moving parts made electronic calculators much faster than their motorized counterparts.

It was the integrated circuit that then made it possible to build hand-held electronic calculators. In comparison to the HP-9100, which required several thousand discrete transistors, the HP-35 depicted in figure 4.11 was built from just five custom integrated circuits. The HP-35 was in many respects a *shrunk* version of the HP-9100 (comparable in size to the Friden SRW calculator shown in figure 4.10). Some hand-held

Figure 4.11. The HP-35 scientific calculator. To miniaturize the calculator Hewlett-Packard used a light-emitting diode (LED) display that showed the contents of only one register. Although LED displays were common in early hand-held calculators, they were eventually replaced by the more energy-efficient liquid crystal display (LCD). This contributed to battery life and hence to further miniaturization of the hand-held calculator.

calculators, such as the Bowmar 901 or the Texas Instruments TI-2500 Datamath, were limited to the four basic arithmetic operations of addition, subtraction, multiplication, and division. However, models like the HP-35, which were known as *scientific calculators*, were also popular early on. These units were capable of performing all of the functions of an engineering slide rule (including computing square roots, exponentials, logarithms, and trigonometric functions) in addition to the four basic arithmetic operations. Given the substantial price of early hand-held calculators, those who first purchased them were scientists and engineers who could use the calculator as a daily tool in their workplace.

The cost of integrated circuits declined rapidly thereafter, and with it, the cost of hand-held calculators. Many recent calculators are built using a single custom integrated circuit, often with substantial quantities of random access memory (RAM) fabricated directly onto the chip. These new chips have made it possible to manufacture, on the one hand, cheap, solar-powered calculators that can cost as little as $5 apiece. On the other hand, there is now a wide range of hand-held devices that have integrated calendars, address books, e-mail, and even general computing capabilities along with the functions of a calculator. In many respects, earlier concerns about cost and product engineering have given way to issues of ergonomics and product design. Like other electrical products with embedded processors, calculators have served as a launching point for an array of products designed to fit various niches in people's daily lives.

FOR FURTHER READING

George C. Chase, "History of Mechanical Computing Machinery," *Annals of the History of Computing* 2 (1980): 198–226.

Edwin Darby, *It All Adds Up—The Growth of Victor Comptometer Corporation* (Chicago, Ill.: Victor Comptometer Corporation, 1968), p. 29.

Chuck House, "Hewlett-Packard and Personal Computing Systems," in Adele Goldberg, ed., *A History of Personal Workstations* (New York: ACM Press, 1988), pp. 401–437.

Ernst Martin, *The Calculating Machines (Die Rechenmaschinen): Their History and Development*, translated and edited by P. A. Kidwell and M. R. Williams (Cambridge, Mass.: MIT Press, 1992).

Michael R. Williams, *A History of Computing Technology* (Englewood Cliffs, N.J.: Prentice-Hall, 1985).

5

The Early Computers

Atsushi Akera

Few aspects of life remained untouched by World War II. Even before the attack on Pearl Harbor, the United States began to mobilize the nation's scientific and engineering resources, particularly through the efforts of the National Defense Research Committee (NDRC). However, the NDRC was not the only vehicle for science mobilization. Many of the armed services, including the U.S. Army Ordnance Department's Ballistic Research Laboratory, made its own arrangements to work with industrial and academic research facilities. Among other things, the Ballistic Research Laboratory (BRL) was charged with producing artillery range tables for the ever-changing kinds of field artillery developed during the war. Taxed beyond its own resources, BRL made an arrangement with the University of Pennsylvania's Moore School of Electrical Engineering to have them help with the work of producing these "firing tables." Some of the work carried out at the Moore School was done on a differential analyzer that was modeled after the unit built by Vannevar Bush at MIT (see chapter 1). A team of skilled women produced the remaining tables using desktop calculating machines. As mentioned in the previous chapter, it was the inability of the Moore School to meet its production schedules using older techniques and machinery that gave John Mauchly and J. Presper Eckert an opportunity to build the Electronic Numerical Integrator And Computer (ENIAC).

While the ENIAC was an impressive new technology, few people realize the extent to which its design was based on older techniques. One technical antecedent was the differential analyzer, which again was already being used to produce ballistic tables. In a manner analogous to the differential analyzer, the ENIAC was designed to perform its calculation by passing values back and forth between many different functional units including 20 accumulators (see figure 5.1) and a high-speed multiplier. Given the different principles of operation, the ENIAC passed these values through a system of plugs and wires rather than rotating mechanical shafts.

Another important antecedent was the mathematical knowledge associated with doing ballistics calculations. Unlike the differential analyzer, which was basically set up to directly emulate the mathematical properties of a ballistic trajectory, the ENIAC had to compute the trajectory through a process of numerical calculation and approximation. Although this was a subtle difference, the numerical approaches to the problem were based on a particular field of mathematics known as *analysis*. A faculty member at the University of Chicago developed the basic

Figure 5.1. The ENIAC was a large-scale, general-purpose digital electronic computer. Built out of some 17,468 electronic vacuum tubes, the ENIAC in its time was the single largest electronic apparatus in the world. The machine was laid out in a U-shaped format around the edge of the room. In addition to special units like the master programmer, the ENIAC did most of its calculations using 20 "accumulators," each of which could hold and add 10-digit numbers at a rate of 5,000 additions/second. The photograph also shows operators checking a program set up using the ENIAC's programming system of switches and plug boards. Courtesy of The University of Pennsylvania Archives.

technique of applying analysis to ballistics calculations quite early on. The general subject of analysis, meanwhile, was a regular part of the college mathematics curriculum, including the curriculum at many women's colleges. It was for this reason that the Moore School could hire women to supervise and perform ballistics calculations during the war. The regular use of these techniques at the Moore School made it easier to assess how to design the ENIAC to perform such calculations. Mauchly and Eckert also drew upon earlier work on electronic calculating devices.

While some people regard the ENIAC as a machine designed to perform ballistics calculations, its inventors (along with their contemporaries) were aware of the broader possibilities of such machines. John Mauchly considered designing a general programming mechanism that would offer a more versatile machine. His own research interests in meteorology and cryptography tended to draw him away from a machine designed only to calculate ballistic tables. Still, it was the exigencies of war that produced the manual method of programming based on switches and plug boards. While this made ENIAC difficult to program, it posed no immediate difficulty because of the repetitive nature of ballistic tables work.

The ENIAC was not completed in time for the war effort. However, between November 1945 and January 1946 it performed significant work by calculating the feasibility of the "Classic" Super, one of the early, experimental designs for the hydrogen bomb. The ENIAC was then dedicated in February 1946 amidst much fanfare. The machine was moved to the Ballistic Research Laboratory shortly thereafter. A number of women who were trained to compute ballistics and to operate the differential analyzer were among the early ENIAC programmers. They transferred their mathematical knowledge and skills to the new machine to become programming experts who could assist other researchers who sought to use the ENIAC.

The EDVAC Report

In many respects, the origins of modern computing can be tied to one report rather than any single machine. The ENIAC laid an important technical foundation by demonstrating the feasibility of computing at full, electronic speeds. As indicated by its use for the hydrogen bomb, the machine drew the attention of nuclear physicists and applied mathematicians who also made substantial advances during the war. Among those drawn to the new machine was the research mathematician, John von Neumann. The war allowed von Neumann to become an important consultant to the military on such phenomena as explosives, shock waves, and general weapons systems design.

Once it became clear that electronic computers would be valuable to military and scientific work, the Army agreed to support a series of meetings between von Neumann and the Moore School staff for the purpose of designing a new machine called the Electronic Discrete Variable Automatic Computer (EDVAC). It is clear that prior to the first meeting in fall of 1944, both Eckert and Mauchly were already exploring different means of programming the machine. Eckert was also working on a new device, the "mercury delay line memory," so that the next computer could store more than the twenty 10-digit numbers that could be stored on the ENIAC. Although much has been made in the historical literature over the "stored-program concept," the idea itself emerged quite early. Key elements of the concept were already in place. The specific decision to store programs as data resulted more from a practical design consideration that such a scheme would obviate the need to build a separate memory system to store a computer program. The rest of the meetings throughout the winter and following spring were dedicated to other engineering tradeoffs and design issues.

Given his formal skills and prominence, John von Neumann was asked to summarize their analysis of the "logical control" of a new machine. But in spite of the joint effort, von Neumann's "First Draft of a Report on the EDVAC" carries the mark of von Neumann's mathematical expertise (see figure 5.2). Using the elegance of a more formal language, von Neumann summarized the different tradeoffs associated with the various components of a computer system. He also devised a system of notation that made it easier to explain what an order code (an "instruction" or "command" in modern programming languages) was within a stored-program design. Whoever contributed the specific ideas, it was this overall description of a new generation of computers that received wide acclaim— at least among the mathematicians who held much of the authority over postwar computer development work. Von Neumann's report became the "blueprint" for the first generation of electronic computers.

The SSEC and other Transitional Machines

Not all postwar efforts were directed towards building a stored-program computer. The ENIAC had substantial downtime, and all of the groups that set out to build a stored-program computer encountered technical difficulties. Individual researchers continued to believe that there were various kinds of mathematical problems for which it was not necessary

First Draft of a Report
on the EDVAC

by

John von Neumann

Contract No. W-670-ORD-4926

Between the

United States Army Ordnance Department

and the

University of Pennsylvania

Moore School of Electrical Engineering
University of Pennsylvania

June 30, 1945

Figure 5.2. Title page from John von Neumann's "First Draft of a Report on the EDVAC." Although this report contained many of the fundamental ideas for the stored-program computer, other design ideas were issued in a subsequent series of reports written by von Neumann and his colleagues at the Institute for Advanced Studies. Courtesy of ENIAC Museum, University of Pennsylvania School of

to perform all of the work at electronic speeds. This was especially true of many applications, including many scientific ones, that required inputting and outputting a large amount of data. The earlier work on mathematical tables (see chapter 1), which Harvard University's Howard Aiken was so proud of, fell into this category.

Those who were convinced that electronic computers would not be around for some time chose to build transitional machines. One such machine was built in 1948 by IBM, the Selective Sequence Electronic Calculator (see figure 5.3). Howard Aiken's third machine, the Harvard Mark III, was also a hybrid machine that combined vacuum tubes with electrical relays. Among others who sought to design such machines was Samuel Caldwell, the Director of MIT's Center for Analysis. After the war, Caldwell organized a design study where he hoped to weigh the benefits of older techniques against the new technology. He aimed to design a machine whose simplicity and economy was suited to the needs of actual computing work.

As mentioned in chapter 4, another important set of transitional machines was the series of electronic calculators built by IBM. Like other transitional machines, their performance was limited by the rate at which both data and instructions could be sent to an electronic arithmetic unit. Still, the IBM 603, IBM 604, and the IBM Card Programmed Electronic Calculator (IBM CPC) served as important workhorses

Figure 5.3. A publicity photo of the Selective Sequence Electronic Calculator (SSEC). The machine is actually part of the walls of this room with the operator's console and data input/output equipment in the center of the room. Some of the paper tape reading mechanisms can be seen at the back of the room. The electronics for control purposes are on the left, while the arithmetic circuits and the machine's limited memory are on the right. The SSEC was used heavily between 1948 and 1951. After IBM developed their own line of commercial computers, the SSEC was dismantled and replaced in this showcase room by an IBM 701. Courtesy of IBM Archives.

for Southern California's aviation industry, as well as Los Alamos and other important research facilities.

One-of-a-Kind Machines

However, most postwar machine development efforts were directed towards the stored-program computer. All of the efforts followed the basic lines of von Neumann's draft report. This included a group von Neumann himself set up at the Institute for Advanced Studies in Princeton, N.J. Eckert and Mauchly left the Moore School shortly after the war to form the Electronic Controls Company, which was formally incorporated as the Eckert-Mauchly Computer Corporation in 1948. There were many other efforts. One of the most ambitious was Jay Forrester's effort at MIT to build a special aircraft design simulator based on a stored-program computer.

These projects fell into two camps. One, based more directly on the EDVAC report, employed the mercury delay-line memory, and followed von Neumann's initial suggestion that a machine perform everything, including its calculation, one bit at a time. This was seen as one way of reducing the reliability problem, since performing the arithmetic in "serial" required fewer vacuum tubes. The UNIVAC I, built by Eckert and Mauchly, and the Standards Eastern Automatic Computer (SEAC), built at the National Bureau of Standards, were both of this variety. The other camp chose a different kind of memory system based on the cathode-ray tube (CRT), which is the same basic component used for television screens. The mercury delay-line stored data as acoustic signals within a tank of mercury. Therefore the signal had to propagate through the length of the tank before it could be read once more as data. By comparison, a CRT-type memory, like the magnetic core memory, which was developed later (see figure 3.1), allows a computer to obtain data directly from any of its memory locations. This device also suggested that a more powerful computer could be built if it handled all of the bits of a number (or an instruction) simultaneously. Von Neumann's own machine at the IAS, along with Forrester's machine at MIT (see figure 5.4), were built of this so-called parallel design.

Yet despite the early U.S. lead, the first two stored-program computers were built in the United Kingdom. While both were relatively modest machines, there was a straightforward integration between the mathematical and engineering aims of the British projects that pushed their work forward more rapidly. In comparison, U.S. projects were plagued by overambitious goals, diffuse research interests, and financial difficulties.

Figure 5.4. In comparison to the Manchester Mark I (see figure 5.5) Jay Forrester's "preprototype" computer, which eventually became the Whirlwind I, occupied more than 70 circuit racks. The scale of this machine and the project's lavish funding reflected the U.S. environment for postwar military research. The size of the machine did not appreciably improve or detract from the machine's capabilities. While the Whirlwind was overengineered in many ways, the project allowed Forrester to think more broadly about the military and strategic possibilities of the new technology. Courtesy of the MITRE Corporation Archives.

The Eckert-Mauchly Computer Corporation was also slowed down by its need to design commercially viable machines. The British also drew upon their own mathematical and cryptographic work during World War II, which included substantial work on specialized electronic computing circuitry. The first machine to be completed was the Manchester Mark I, a limited prototype computer built at the University of Manchester in 1948 (see figure 5.5). Maurice Wilkes built a more useful machine at Cambridge University in 1949.

Computers in the Market

It took a while for computers to reach the market. In comparison to the machines built at Manchester and Cambridge, machines like Eckert and Mauchly's UNIVAC I had to be designed to serve a wide range of

Figure 5.5. The first operational stored-program computer was the Manchester Mark I, built at the University of Manchester in 1948. Because this was a prototype built to test out the stored-program concept, it was very limited in its ability. Its memory would store only 32 numbers or instructions, and the machine could only subtract or compare two numbers. One of the Mark I's other important functions was to test the British Williams Tube memory. Although all CRT-type memories were fickle, the British tube proved to be one of the most reliable designs. Reprinted with permission of the Department of Computer Science, University of Manchester.

applications. They also had to be built to withstand the rigors of regular operation, and be maintained by specially trained customer engineers rather than the engineers who built the machines. The first UNIVAC I was released in June of 1951, and delivered shortly thereafter to the U.S. Census Bureau.

Although the UNIVAC had an initial lead, IBM quickly came to dominate the market during the mid-1950s. While there are various accounts of IBM's dominance, perhaps the most compelling explanation is the notion of an installed base, as suggested most recently by historians Martin Campbell-Kelly and William Aspray. For most businesses, computing was less about computers than the corporate procedures like accounting and inventory that were associated with them. The market for punched card machinery was already dominated by IBM, and few firms were willing to try a new manufacturer when they could adapt their existing system to accommodate the new electronic technology. Even within the domain of scientific and engineering computation, several dozen facilities were already making use of IBM equipment, including the IBM 602A, IBM 604, and IBM CPC, when UNIVAC was first released. Product loyalty had already been earned by IBM among its scientific users, so that its stored-program computers—the IBM 701, IBM 704, and IBM 650—also captured this market (see figure 5.6).

Figure 5.6. The IBM 705, which was closely related to the IBM 704. As with the SSEC, the computer's presentation was always a major consideration. Although vacuum tubes were at the heart of these machines, the boxes containing the computing circuitry were often placed in the rear of the room. The casual visitor would normally see an operator's console along with an impressive array of magnetic tapes. Courtesy of IBM Archives.

Integration and Diversity

As described by Brian Randell in chapter 3, the 1960s was a decade that saw a simultaneous trend toward integration and diversity. By the late 1950s, IBM had clear dominance in the market. However, with new manufacturers entering the market, including the industrial giant General Electric, IBM made a move to consolidate their position. Considered a "five billion dollar gamble" by some, this was an effort to offer a new integrated product line designed to serve both small and large users. Six different machines were announced by IBM for its new System/360 series in April of 1964 (see figure 5.7). The claim that these would be upward and downward compatible machines—programs written for any machine could be run on another except for limitations of memory and mass storage—was based as much on advances in computer programming as on computer hardware. Specifically, downward compatibility was based on the principle that smaller computers in the product line would support through computer subroutines those instructions not supported in hardware.

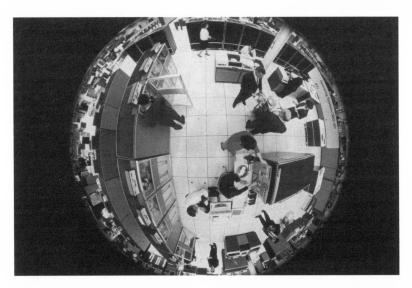

Figure 5.7. The IBM System 360/40. Although IBM initially offered different computers for their business and scientific users (e.g., the IBM 702 and 705 as opposed to the IBM 701 and 704), by the late 1950s it was already clear that there was little difference between these two kinds of users. The one substantial difference was the scientist and engineer's need to compute floating-point numbers (numbers of the form, 7.2159). By offering floating-point hardware as a special option, the System/360 also integrated IBM's scientific and commercial product lines. Courtesy of IBM Archives.

Yet despite IBM's best effort, the 1960s saw an increasingly diverse range of computer equipment. At the one end, minicomputers, beginning with the Digital Equipment Corporation's PDP-1, were installed in many scientific, engineering, and medical research facilities (see figure 5.8). Just like the subsequent popularity of the electronic calculator, smaller machines, irrespective of their price–performance ratio, were often more suited to the work practices of many researchers. Supercomputers occupied the other end (see figure 5.9). These machines were designed to support the work of nuclear weapons development, cryptography, and the most demanding of scientific calculations. It was not by accident that the equipment offered by new manufacturers was the most popular among technical users. Scientists and engineers often used their machines for very specific aims, and therefore knowing how to configure both hardware and software was part of their expertise. These users were less dependent on the standard software and service arrangements provided by IBM.

Other computers were sold as part of industrial control equipment and as a part of military command and control systems. Various firms also

Figure 5.8. Digital Equipment Corporation's PDP-8 was a highly popular early minicomputer. It was only with the introduction of the minicomputer that larger computers, including the entire System/360 line, came to be known as "mainframe" computers. Courtesy of Compaq Computers.

Figure 5.9. Seymour Cray with the Cray I "supercomputer," ca. 1974. Although IBM also tried to build supercomputers beginning with the IBM 7030 "Stretch" computer in 1960, other firms such as Cray Research and Control Data Corporation surpassed IBM in building the most powerful computers out of the most advanced components available at the time. Courtesy of the Charles Babbage Institute, University of Minnesota, Minneapolis.

Figure 5.10. Although the von Neumann architecture continued to dominate commercially built machines, various efforts were made to build computers with a different underlying design. One of the earliest of these was the ILLIAC IV, built at the University of Illinois. Courtesy of the Charles Babbage Institute, University of Minnesota, Minneapolis.

set out to develop computer timesharing systems. These systems were especially important to central academic computing facilities, which had to serve the needs of as many as several thousand users. Still, the basic "von Neumann architecture" continued to dominate nearly all computer designs (regarding exceptions, see figure 5.10). And while IBM conceded some of the new niche markets to its competitors, it continued to dominate the overall sales of digital computers.

FOR FURTHER READING

Martin Campbell-Kelly and William Aspray, *Computer: A History of the Information Machine* (New York: Basic Books, 1996).

Tracy Kidder, *The Soul of a New Machine* (New York: Avon Books, 1981).

Emerson Pugh, *Building IBM: Shaping an Industry and Its Technology* (Cambridge, Mass.: MIT Press, 1995).

Michael R. Williams, *A History of Computing Technology,* second edition (Los Alamitos, Calif.: IEEE Computer Society Press, 1998).

6

Pioneers in Computing

J. A. N. Lee

$\mathbf{T}$ake three computer historians and put them in a room to develop a wallchart on the history of computing and you will find that they each have a differing view of the underlying chronology. One will gear his views to the sequence of machines that epitomize the development of the computer from the abacus to the PC; the second will concentrate on the concepts of computation perhaps starting from the birth of numbers and then algorithms up to the programming languages of today. I would tend to side with the third historian who would believe that the history of computing is the built on the backs of the pioneers of computing, without whose insights and innovations there would be no machines and no algorithms. These are the men and women of computing who "dared to fail" and in the process discovered ideas that changed the face of computing.

In my teaching of the history of computing I like to start with John Napier, Laird of Merchiston (1550–1617), the developer of logarithms, the "bones" that bear his name, a (binary) chessboard computer, and the promptuary.[1] It has long amazed me that the small country of Scotland could produce so many visionaries and artists when it was in a constant battle for its life. The rugged hills and mountains do not seem to be the appropriate cradle for provoking thoughts of machines and painting vistas through poetry and narrative. Napier used much of his scientific study in the simplification of the problem of multiplication, a problem whose solution in the 16th century was a measure of the educated man. While logarithms, bones, and promptuary were solutions that outlasted the man, one of his machines was lost quickly, since it did not fit into the environment of the day—the chessboard computer. This machine, easily constructed from a chessboard and chips, demonstrates the binary number system in all the arithmetic operations and is probably the first binary calculator that existed for almost 400 years, until Konrad Zuse chanced on the concept for his first machine.

Blaise Pascal (1623–1666) is our French contributor to this history. Mathematician and philosopher, Pascal invented an adding machine with automatic carry between successive digit positions, as well as the "Pascal Triangle" of coefficients of the binomial series. Son of a tax collector, Pascal was a child prodigy who discovered the proof of Euclid's 32nd Proposition at the age of 12: "la somme des angles d'un triangle quelconque est égale à deux angles droits."[2] Four years later he developed a fundamental theorem of projective geometry, such that the projections of the opposing sides of a hexagon inscribed in a conic section intersect to define a single line named the "droite de Pascal." In assisting his father he became impressed by the need for a mechanical device for performing arithmetic operations and, in 1642, developed his adding (and subtracting) machine. The primary innovation of the calculator was its ability to automatically carry the "tens" digit from one position to the next. During the next decade he built almost 50 copies of the machine, but most of them were used as parlor curiosities of their rich purchasers rather than working machines. Pascal is also credited with the invention of the wheelbarrow, the omnibus, and the roulette wheel. On November 23, 1654, Pascal experienced a religious event that caused him to retire to the hermitage at Port-Royal des Champs where, in later years, he developed what is now known as "Pascal's Wager." He argued that if God does not exist then one loses nothing by believing in him; but if God does exist, one can gain eternal life by believing in him. This argument was in opposition to the then widely held belief in predestination, which in turn rejected the concept of free will. Obviously if one were to choose to believe in God (or not) then that is an expression of free will.

One hundred and fifty years later, Charles Babbage (1791–1871) was a similarly inspired inventor whose contributions go far beyond the field of computing (see figure 6.1). Known to some as the "father of computing" for his contributions to the basic design of the computer through the analytical engine, Babbage is perhaps better known for the difference engine, which was a special-purpose device intended for the production of tables. Babbage is a figure in history who has been maligned for many years as a poor manager, an impractical scientist, and an insensitive publican. Several online biographies of Babbage give the impression that

Figure 6.1. Charles Babbage. Courtsey of the Burndy Library, Dibner Institute for the History of Science and Technology.

Babbage failed in his quest for the computer by designing machines that were beyond the capabilities of the current technology to manufacture. However, his designs were taken and simplified by Georg and Edvard Scheutz to construct the first working devices within Babbage's lifetime. On the bicentenary of the birth of Charles Babbage, the Science Museum (London) took his mechanical drawings for the difference engine, and using 19th century methodologies built the complete difference engine, finding only a few minor errors in his design—errors that would have been easily identified in the time of Babbage. His only significant error, if any, was to be too far-sighted and too eager to take a step forward before he had his other foot firmly planted. The same opportunity occurred during the construction of the ENIAC by J. Presper Eckert and John Mauchly at the University of Pennsylvania in the mid-1940s. They realized during construction that a better machine could be created by installing a stored memory system, but their decision was to complete the current machine, deliver it to their sponsor, and then adapt it later to the improved technology. Babbage hated street musicians, who reacted by playing their instruments outside his house. This antisocial behavior has been touted as characteristic of the man throughout his life, when in fact, he had a physical infirmity that triggered his outcries against street music. In 1991, his great-grandson, Neville Babbage, himself a physician, examined Babbage's autopsy report and noted that his ancestor had calcification of the ear canals, a condition that would have caused pain when subjected to loud noises and probably certain frequencies. Maybe Babbage was antisocial in his later years; he was also in pain.

To my mind, Ada King, Countess of Lovelace (see figure 6.2), has been a much misunderstood character in computer history, much like Babbage. While she has been labeled as the "first programmer in the world" for her work on the notes regarding the analytical engine and for her contributions to the understanding of that machine, it is not at all clear that she had a vision of computation that would solve her problems with gambling and horse racing, if such problems truly existed.

Augusta Ada Byron (1815–1852), was the daughter of the poet Lord Byron, though her parents separated when Ada was quite young and her upbringing was supervised by her mother. Apparently Lady Byron had a fear that Ada might take to poetry and thus favor her father. She contrived therefore to push Ada's education in an orthogonal direction by employing tutors with a mathematical bent. One of those was Augustus De Morgan (1806–1871, famous in logic for De Morgan's law). In 1834, through her

Figure 6.2. Lady Ada King, Countess of Lovelace, from an 1835 painting by Margaret Carpenter. Courtsey of the Institute of Electrical and Electronics Engineers (IEEE), Inc.

friendship with Mary Summerville, she first met Charles Babbage, who invited her to visit his home and to view his engines. Ada was intrigued by Babbage's inventions, and undertook a correspondence with him so as to extend her learning even further. Shortly thereafter Ada married William King, soon to become the Earl of Lovelace. Fortunately her husband did not oppose her friendship with Babbage or her interest in mathematics and machines.

Through this association with Babbage, Ada came to learn of the article by Count Menabrea on the analytical engine, offering to translate it into English. Encouraged by Babbage, she not only completed the translation but also added notes of her own, which in magnitude exceeded the word count of the original article. Ada published the resulting paper in Richard Taylor's Scientific Memoirs series. Within her notes she saw the potential for repeated actions through iteration, which she likened to a snake eating its own tail, and foresaw the need for conditional branching. Using her perhaps genetic powers of poetry she also likened the sets of instructions to a poem, presumably seeing the syntactic format of poetry as an analog to the format of programs. In 1852, after a long illness, Ada died in pain and was buried alongside her father in Nottinghamshire, the first time that she had been close to him.

An examination of the period of the 1930s clearly shows that the technology of computation, mechanical calculating, and digital electronics had progressed to the point where there was sufficient capability for the development of the concept of the computer. For the time being we will argue over the appropriate attribution of the "inventor of the computer," choosing primarily among John V. Atanasoff, Konrad Zuse, Howard Aiken, George Stibitz, and Alan Turing. Working independently and in highly disparate environments, these five men essentially discovered or developed the underpinnings of the computer as we know it today.

John V. Atanasoff (1903–1995) had a great interest in mathematics from an early age. When about 10 years old, he was curious about a Dietzgen slide rule that his father had bought. John Vincent read the instructions on how to use the slide rule, and he became more interested in the mathematical principles of the slide rule. In later years, after completing his doctorate at the University of Wisconsin and taking up a position at Iowa State College (now University), he replaced the analog concepts of the slide rule with digital concepts, and married that notion with the then developing ideas of electronics. Atanasoff developed four important concepts:

1. He would use electricity and electronics as the medium for the computer.

2. In spite of custom, he would use base-two numbers (the binary system) for his computer.
3. He would use condensers for memory and would use a regenerative or "jogging" process to avoid lapses that might be caused by leakage of power.
4. He would compute by direct logical action and not by enumeration as used in analog calculating devices.

Though restricting his innovations to the solution of one particular problem, that of solving simultaneous linear equations, he built a machine, with the assistance of Clifford Berry, a graduate assistant, that contained the elements of the modern computer. Regrettably he was never able to move the machine out of the laboratory, and thus his ideas lay dormant until the late 1960s.

During this same period, Konrad Zuse, a civil engineer by training and an aeronautical engineer by employment, recognized the need for a better means of performing computations (see figure 6.3). Ensconced in his parent's parlor, Zuse built the first of a series of machines that also incorporated the accepted components of a modern computer using relay technology. He immediately saw that this machine would be unsatisfactory as a production model, and with the help of Helmut Schreyer envisaged the electronic version of the computer. Like Atanasoff, Zuse developed his own set of strategies for his machines. Each machine would operate:

1. under program control,
2. with the binary system of numbers,
3. and using floating point arithmetic,

which in turn would necessitate:

1. allowing fully automatic arithmetical calculation,
2. with a high-capacity memory,
3. and modules or relays operating on the yes/no principle.

The first fully functional program-controlled electromechanical digital computer in the world (initially named the Z3) was completed by Zuse in 1941, but was destroyed in 1944 during the war. Because of its historical importance, a copy was made in 1960 and put on display in the German Museum ("Deutsches Museum") in Munich. In 1941, Zuse proposed that the Nazi government support the production of these machines, but was rebuffed on the basis that his time to completion (estimated at two years) was beyond the wartime needs of the Third Reich. The war would be over before the task was completed.

Figure 6.3. Konrad Zuse. Courtsey of the Institute of Electrical and Electronics Engineers (IEEE), Inc.

Next came the more sophisticated Z4, which was the only Zuse machine to survive the war. At this time, Zuse redesignated his machines as the Z-series, in order to obviate the confusion with the V-weapons of the later years of World War II. The Z4 was almost complete when, due to continued air raids, it was moved from Berlin to Gottingen, where it was installed in the laboratory of the Aerodynamische Versuchanstalt (DVL, an Experimental Aerodynamics Institute). It was only there for a few weeks before Gottingen was in danger of being captured and the machine was once again moved to a small village, Hinterstein, in the Allgau/Bavaria. Finally, it was taken to Switzerland where it was installed in the ETH (Eidgenossisch Technische Hochschule, Federal Polytechnical Institute) in Zurich in 1950. It was used in the Institute of Applied Mathematics at the ETH until 1955.

Over the years, Zuse continually reassessed the capabilities of his machines, and claimed in several biographical presentations to have incorporated the stored-program concept, programming languages, and object-oriented programming in his devices. There is no doubt that Zuse had many of the ideas that were later to be credited to others, but his location in occupied Germany, and later in Switzerland, prevented others from viewing his work until much later.

Parallel with Atanasoff and Zuse, Howard Aiken (1900–1973) at Harvard University felt the same urge to replace tedious hand computation, even when done by human computers, by a more mechanical means. Basing his design for such a device on the established designs for calculators, he approached the Munroe Calculating Company to implement his ideas. Linking a gregarious set of calculators together did not seem to fit the vision of the company, and thus Aiken was forced to redirect his attention to IBM. With assistance from Harvard colleagues, and a modification of his design to fit better into the card processing style of IBM's line of machines, he found a willing partner in Thomas J. Watson, Sr., and the staff of the Endicott plant in New York State. Though Aiken's plans had been born in the mid-1930s, it was not until 1943 that the machine was completed. It was delivered to Harvard University in 1944. It was then set to work on problems for the U.S. Navy. Named the Automatic Sequence Controlled Calculator (ASCC) by IBM, it was designated as the Harvard Mark I by Aiken. He followed that machine with three others, built at Harvard under his direct supervision. The Harvard Mark III was particularly significant in that it contained the first magnetic drum and had a stored program.

In a 1972 interview, Aiken predicted that by the year 2000, computer companies would be giving away computers in order to sell their software. Interestingly enough, on September 17, 1997, Netscape announced that they would be providing free computers in order to promote their World Wide Web browser sales!

In the fall of 1937, while an engineer at Bell Telephone Laboratories, George Stibitz (1904–1995) used surplus relays, tin-can strips, flashlight bulbs, and other canonical items to construct his "Model K" (for Kitchen table) breadboard digital calculator, which could add two bits and display the result (see figure 6.4). A replica of this device is now on display at

Figure 6.4. George R. Stibitz (center).

the Smithsonian Institution. Bell Telephone Laboratories recognized a potential solution to the problem of high-speed complex-number calculation, which was holding back contemporary development of wide-area telephone networks. By late 1938, the laboratory had authorized development of a full-scale relay calculator on the Stibitz model; Stibitz and his design team began construction in April 1939. The end product, known as the Complex Number Calculator, first ran on January 8, 1940. Later that year during a meeting of the American Mathematical Society at Dartmouth College, Stibitz used a Teletype to transmit problems to the Complex Number Calculator and receive the computed results. This is now generally considered the world's first example of remote job entry, a technique that would revolutionize dissemination of information through telephone and computer networks. Throughout the war years, Stibitz continued to develop bigger and better versions of the relay calculator as the Laboratory's contribution to the war effort. However, on the cessation of fighting, Bell Telephone Laboratories turned their attention inwards, and while they built more Stibitz machines, they were targeted toward their own business and not to general-purpose computing.

Alan Turing (1912–1954) developed an aptitude for the sciences early in his school life. When it came to the more "right brain" topics of English and history, however, his attention waned. His instructors attempted to convince him to study other disciplines, but he would respond only to mathematics and science. He retained this trait throughout his education.

He began his career in mathematics at King's College, Cambridge University, in 1931. Turing seemed to have little interest in using the work of previous scientists; he would typically spend time recreating their work instead. Upon graduation, Turing was made a fellow of King's College, and then moved on to Princeton University. It was during this time that he explored what was later called the "Turing Machine."

Turing helped pioneer the concept of the digital computer. He described a machine that would read a series of symbols from an unbounded tape. The machine described the steps that needed to be done to solve a particular problem or perform a certain task based on the manipulation of the symbols on the tape. The Turing Machine would read each of the steps and perform them in an appropriate order, resulting in the desired answer.

This concept was revolutionary for the time. What Turing envisioned was a machine that could do anything, something that we take for granted today. The method of instructing the computer was very important in Turing's concept. He essentially described a machine that supported only a few simple instructions. Making the computer perform a particular task was simply a matter of breaking the job down into a series of these simple instructions. This is identical to the process programmers go through today. He believed that an algorithm could be developed for most any problem. The hard part was determining what the simple steps were and how to break down the larger problems. Satisfied that his concepts provided the foundation for describing "computation," and in particular "computability," Turing turned his theory into practice in a production machine. He would, however, use these concepts in the development of the first electronic computer in the United Kingdom.

During World War II, Turing used his knowledge and ideas in the Department of Communications of the Foreign Office of Great Britain. Working at Bletchley Park in central England, he used his mathematical skills to decipher the codes the German armed forces were using to communicate. This was an especially difficult task because the Germans had developed a type of encoder called the Enigma. It was able to generate a constantly changing code that was thought to be impossible for the code breakers to decipher in a timely fashion. Through this work, the Bletchley Park decoders were able to give sufficient information to the Royal Navy to win the Battle of the Atlantic, and to further the cause of the war effort in North Africa. Following the construction of several specialized machines, Turing and his fellow scientists developed a special-purpose device called Colossus. This quickly and efficiently deciphered the German codes created by the high-level encoding devices. Built by engineers at the Telephone Research Establishment, lead by Tommy Flowers, the Colossus was influential in supporting the intelligence needed for the prosecution of D-Day and the subsequent actions that led to the end of the war. Following the war, Colossus and its several copies were destroyed as part of the perceived need for continued secrecy, and the secret of the machine died for over 25 years. Thus the Colossus had no direct impact on the development of the computer in the United Kingdom.

After World War II, Turing went on to work for the National Physical Laboratory (NPL) and continued his research into digital computers. Here he worked on developing the Automatic Computing Engine (ACE), one of the first attempts at creating a true digital computer. It was during this time that he began to explore the relationship between computers and nature. He wrote a paper called "Intelligent Machinery," which was not published until 1969, years after his death. This was one of the first times the concept of artificial intelligence was raised. The ACE was built by others at NPL and eventually became the prototype for a series of machines built by the English Electric Company.

Turing believed that machines could be created that would mimic the processes of the human brain. He discussed the possibility of such machines, and acknowledged the difficulty people would have accepting a machine that would rival their own intelligence. This is a problem that still plagues artificial intelligence today. In his mind, there was nothing the brain could do that a well-designed computer could not. As part of his argument, Turing described devices already in existence that worked like parts of the human body, such as television cameras and microphones.

If we celebrate the 100th anniversary of the computer, and tie it to the unveiling of the ENIAC in 1946, as was the case for the 50th anniversary, it will be difficult to look back and distinguish it from the work of the five men—Atanasoff, Zuse, Aiken, Stibitz, and Turing—that preceded it with any serious degree of discrimination. Preceding the work of John Mauchly and J. Presper Eckert by almost a decade, their work set the stage for the evolution of the computer (see figure 6.5). They proved that the pieces of the pie were all there ready to be assembled into "The Machine that Changed the World." Mauchly and Eckert brought these pieces all together in a machine that had a prominent place in the environment of the day, with a university and sponsor that were willing

Figure 6.5. J. Presper Eckert. Courtsey of the Institute of Electrical and Electronics Engineers (IEEE), Inc.

to put in the effort at public relations that was needed to show the public that their money had been well spent. The ENIAC was not the machine that changed the world, instead it was the machine that spawned the ideas that showed what that machine should look like and how it should behave. The continued work of Eckert and Mauchly in setting up the world's first computer company, and delivering one of the first commercial machines, was highly influential in placing the computer at the hub of the postwar world. UNIVAC became the synonym for computer in the 1950s, only to be overtaken by IBM and then the PC, in succession.

NOTES

1. See my book *Computer Pioneers* (Los Alamitos, Calif.: IEEE Computer Society Press, 1955).
2. "The sum of the angles of any triangle equals two right angles."

FOR FURTHER READING

Cortada, James W. *Historical Dictionary of Data Processing: Biographies* (Westport, Conn.: Greenwood Press, 1987).

Lee, J. A. N. *Computer Pioneers* (Los Alamitos, Calif.: IEEE Computer Society Press, 1995).

Slater, Robert. *Portraits in Silicon* (Cambridge, Mass.: MIT Press, 1987).

II

Software

7

Software: The Self-Programming Machine

Michael S. Mahoney

In May 1973, *Datamation* published a Rand report filed six months earlier by Barry Boehm and based on studies undertaken by the Air Force Systems Command, which was concerned about the growing mismatch between its needs and its resources in the design and development of computer-based systems. Titled "Software and Its Impact: A Quantitative Assessment," the article attached numbers to the generally shared sense of malaise in the industry: software was getting more and more costly. Drawing on various empirical studies of programming and programmers undertaken in the late 1960s, Boehm tried to indicate where to look for relief by disaggregating the costs into the major stages of software projects. Perhaps the most striking visualization of the problem was a graph with a flattened logistic curve illustrating the inversion of the relative costs of hardware and software over the 30-year period 1955–85. Whereas software had constituted less than 20% of the cost of a system in 1955, current trends suggested that it would make up over 90% by 1985. At the time of Boehm's study, software's share already stood at 75%.

Boehm's article belongs to the larger issue of the "software crisis" and the origins of software engineering, to which I shall return presently, but for the moment it also serves to make a historiographical point. Software development has remained a labor-intensive activity, an art rather than a science. Indeed, that is what computer people have found so troublesome and some have tried to remedy. Boehm's figures show that by 1970 some three-quarters of the productive energies of the computer industry were going into software. By then at the latest, the history of computing had become the history of software.

At present the literature of the history of computing does not reflect that fact. Except perhaps for the major programming languages, the story of software has been largely neglected. The history of areas such as operating systems, databases, graphics, and real-time and interactive computing still lies in past survey articles, prefaces of textbooks, and retrospectives by the people involved. When one turns from systems software to applications programming, the gap widens. Applications, after all, are what make the computer worth having; without them a computer is of no more utility or value than a television set without broadcasting. James Cortada has provided a start toward a history of applications through his quite useful bibliographic guide, but there are only a few studies of only the largest and most famous programs (SAGE, SABRE, ERMA, etc.). We have practically no historical accounts of how, starting in the early 1950s, government, business, and industry put their operations on the computer. Aside from a few studies with a primarily sociological focus in the 1970s, programming as a new technical activity and programmers as a new labor force have received no historical attention. Except for very recent studies of the origins and development of the Internet, we have no substantial histories of the word processor, the spreadsheet, communications, or the other software on which the personal computer industry and some of the nation's largest personal fortunes rest.

Software, then, presents a huge territory awaiting historical exploration, with only a few guideposts by which to maintain one's bearings. One guiding principle in particular seems clear: if application software is about getting the computer to do something useful in the world, systems software is about getting the computer to do the applications programming. It is the latter theme that I shall mainly pursue here. Eventually, I shall come back to applications programming by way of software engineering, but only insofar as it touches on the main theme.

Programming Computers

Basically, programming is a simple, logical procedure, but as the problems to be solved grow, the labor of programming also increases, and the aid of the computer is enlisted to devise its own programs.

Werner Buchholz

The idea of programs that write programs is inherent in the concept of the universal Turing machine, set forth by Alan M. Turing in 1936. He showed that any computation can be described in terms of a machine shifting among a finite number of states in response to a sequence of symbols read and written one at a time on a potentially infinite tape. Since the description of the machine can itself be expressed as a sequence of symbols, Turing went on to describe a universal machine that can read the description of any specific machine and then carry out the computation it describes. The computation in question can very well be a description of a universal Turing machine, a notion which John von Neumann pursued to its logical conclusion in his work on self-replicating automata. As a form of Turing machine, the stored-program computer is in principle a self-programming device, limited in practice by finite memory. That limitation seemed overwhelming at first, but in the mid-1950s, the concept of computer-assisted programming began to meet with striking success in the form of programming languages, programming and operating systems, and databases and report generators.

Indeed, that success emboldened people to think about programming languages and programming environments that would obviate the need for programmers in the long run and in the meantime bring them under increasing effective managerial control. By 1961, Herbert A. Simon was not alone in predicting that,

> We can dismiss the notion that computer programmers will become a powerful elite in the automated corporation. It is far more likely that the programming occupation will become extinct (through the further development of self-programming techniques) than that it will become all powerful. More and more, computers will program themselves; and direction will be given to computers through the mediation of compiling systems that will be completely neutral so far as the content of the decision rules is concerned.[1]

Simon was talking about 1985, yet, in the new millennium, programmers are neither extinct nor even an endangered species. Indeed, old COBOL programmers found renewed life in patching the Y2K problem.

Coincidentally, Simon's remarks were reprinted by John Diebold in 1973, which is just about the point of transition between the successful and the less successful phases of the project of the self-programming computer. By the early 1970s, the basic elements of current systems software were in place, and development efforts since then have been aimed largely at their refinement and extension. With few exceptions, the programming languages covered in the two ACM History of Programming Languages conferences in 1978 and 1993 were conceived before 1975. They include the major languages currently in use for applications and systems programming. In particular, C and Unix both date from the turn of the 1970s, as do IBM's current operating systems.

The graphical user interfaces (GUIs) of Windows and MacOS rest on foundations laid at Stanford in the 1960s and Xerox PARC in the early and mid-1970s. The seminal innovations in both local and wide-area networking also date from that time. Developments since then have built on those foundations.

By 1973, too, "software engineering" was under way as a conscious effort to resolve the problems of producing software on time, within budget, and to specifications. Among the concepts driving that effort, conceived of as a form of industrial engineering, is the "software factory", either on the Taylorist model of "the one best way" of programming enforced by the programming environment or on the Ford model of the assembly line, where automated programming removes the need for enforcement by severely reducing the role of human judgment. At a conference in August 1996 on the history of software engineering, leading figures of the field agreed only that after almost 30 years, whatever form it might eventually take as an engineering discipline, it wasn't one yet. While software development environments have automated some tasks, programming "in the large" remains a labor-intensive form of craft production.

So we can perhaps usefully break systems software up into programming tools and programming environments on the one hand and software development (or, if you prefer, software engineering) on the other. Both fall under the general theme of getting the computer to do the programming. Both have become prerequisites to getting the computer to do something useful.

Programming Tools

It is a commonplace that a computer can do anything for which precise and unambiguous instructions can be given. The difficulties of programming computers seem to have caught their creators by surprise. Werner Buchholz's optimism is counterbalanced by Maurice Wilkes's realization that he would be spending much of his life debugging programs.[2] On a larger scale, companies that introduced computers into their operations faced the problem of communication between the people who knew how the organization worked and those who knew how the computer worked. International Business Machines had built its electrical accounting machinery (EAM) business in large part by providing that mediation through its sales staff, whose job it was to match IBM's equipment to the customer's business. At first it seemed that computers meant little more than changing the "E" in "EAM" from "Electrical" to

"Electronic," but experience soon showed otherwise. Programming the computer proved to be difficult, time-consuming, and error-prone. Even when completed, programs required maintenance in the form of addition of functions not initially specified, adjustment of unanticipated outcomes, and correction of previously undetected mistakes. With each change of computer to a larger or newer model came the need to repeat the programming process from the start, since the old code would not run on the new machine. The situation placed a strain on both the customer and IBM, and together with other manufacturers they therefore shared an interest in means of easing and speeding the task of programming and of making programs compatible with a variety of computers.

In addition to having to work within the confines of the machine's instruction set and hardware protocols, one had to do one's own clerical tasks of assigning variables to memory and of keeping track of the numerical order of the instructions. The last became a systematic problem on Cambridge's Electronic Delay Storage Automatic Calculator (EDSAC) as the notion of a library of subroutines took hold, necessitating the incorporation of the modules at various points in a program. Symbolic assemblers began to appear in the early 1950s, enabling programmers to number instructions provisionally for easy insertion, deletion, and reference and, more important, turning over to the assembler the allocation of memory for symbolically denoted variables.[3] Although symbolic assemblers took over the clerical tasks, they remained tied to the basic instruction set, albeit mnemonic rather than numeric. During the late 1950s, macro assemblers enabled programmers to group sequences of instructions as functions and procedures (with parameters) in forms closer to their own way of thinking and thus to extend the instruction set.

The first high-level programming languages, perhaps most famously FORTRAN in 1957, followed over the next three years by LISP, COBOL, and ALGOL, took a quite different approach to programming by differentiating between the language in which humans think about problems and the language by which the machine is addressed. To the clerical tasks of the assembler, compilers and interpreters added the functions of parsing the syntax and construing the semantics of the human-oriented programming language and translating them into the appropriate sequences of assembler or machine instructions. At first, as with FORTRAN, developers of compilers strove for little more than a program that would fit into the target machine and that would produce reasonably efficient code. Once they had established the practicality of compilers, however, they shifted their goals.

In translating human-oriented languages into machine code, compilers separated programming from the machines on which the programs ran: "ALGOL 60 is the name of a notation for expressing computational processes, irrespective of any particular uses or computer implementations," said one of its creators.[4] Subsequently, the design of programming languages increasingly focused on the forms of computational reasoning best suited to various domains of application, while the design of compilers attended to the issues of accurate translation across a range of machines. With that shift of focus at the turn of the 1960s, the development of programming languages and their compilers converged with research in theoretical computer science, first to establish the general principles underlying lexical analysis and the parsing of formal languages, then to implement those principles in general programs for moving from a formal specification of the vocabulary and grammar of a language to the corresponding lexical analyzer and parser, which not only resolved the source program into its constituents and verified its syntactical correctness but also allowed the incorporation of preset blocks of machine code associated with those constituents to produce the compiler itself. By means of such tools, for example lex and yacc in the Unix system, a compiler that in the late 1950s would have required several staff-years became feasible for a pair of undergraduates in a semester. By contrast, automatic generation of code, or the translation of the abstract terms of the programming language into the concrete instruction set of the target machine, proved more resistant to theoretical understanding (formal semantics) and thus to automation, especially in a form that assured semantic invariance across platforms.

Systems Software

"Problem-oriented languages," as they were called, were designed to facilitate the work of programmers by freeing them from the operational details of the computer or computers on which their programs would run. The more abstract the language, the more it depended on a programming system to supply those details whether through a library of standard routines or through compilers, linkers, and loaders that fitted the program to the mode of operation of the particular computer. Thus software aimed at shielding the programmer from the machine intersected with software, namely operating systems, meant to shield the machine from the programmer.

Operating systems emerged in the mid-1950s, largely out of concerns to enhance the efficiency of computer operations by minimizing nonproductive time between runs. Rather than allowing programmers to set up and run their jobs one by one, the systems enabled operators to load a batch of programs with accompanying instructions for setup and turn them over to a supervisory program to run them and to alert the operators when their intervention was required. With improvements in hardware, the systems expanded to include transfer and allocation of tasks among several processors (multiprocessing), in particular separating slower input/output (I/O) operations from the main computation. At the turn of the 1960s, with the development of techniques for handling communications between processors, multiprogramming systems began running several programs in common memory, switching control back and forth among them according to increasingly sophisticated scheduling algorithms and memory protection schemes.

The development of hardware and software for rapid transfer of data between core and secondary storage essentially removed the limits on the former by mapping it into the latter by segments, or "pages," and swapping them in and out as required by the program currently running. Such a system could then circulate control among a large number of programs, some or all of which could be processes interacting online with users at consoles (timesharing). With each step in this development, applications programmers moved farther down an expanding hierarchy of layers of control that intervened between them and the computer itself. Only the layer at the top corresponded to a real machine; all the rest were virtual machines requiring translation to the layer above. Indeed, in IBM's OS/360 even the top layer was a virtual machine, translated by microprogrammed firmware into the specific instruction sets of the computers making up System/360. Despite appearances of direct control, this layering of abstract machines was as true of interactive systems as of batch systems. It remains true of current personal computing environments, the development of which has for the most part recapitulated the evolution of mainframe systems, adding to them a new layer of graphical user interfaces (GUIs). For example, Windows NT does not allow any application to communicate directly with the basic I/O system (BIOS), thus disabling some DOS and Windows 9x software.

What is important for present purposes about this highly condensed account of a history that remains largely uninvestigated is the extent to which operating systems increasingly realized the ideal of the computer as a self-programming device. In the evolution from the monitors of the mid-1950s to the interactive timesharing systems of the early 1970s, programs themselves became dynamic entities. The programmer specified in abstract terms the structure of the data and the flow of computation. Making those terms concrete became the job of the system software, which in turn relied on increasingly elaborate addressing schemes to vary the specific links in response to run-time conditions. The operating system became the master choreographer in an ever more complex dance of processes, coordinating them to move tightly among one another, singly and in groups, yet without colliding. The task required the development of sophisticated techniques of exception-handling and dynamic data management, but the possibility of carrying it out at all rested ultimately on the computer's capacity to rewrite its own tape.

Software Systems

Having concentrated during the 1960s on programming languages and operating systems as the means of addressing the problems of programming and software, the computing community shifted, or at least split its attention during the following decade. Participants at the 1968 NATO Conference on Software Engineering reinforced each other's growing sense that the cost overruns, slips in schedule, and failure to meet specifications that plagued the development of large-scale and mission-critical software systems reflected a systemic disorder, to be remedied only by placing "software manufacturer ... on the types of theoretical foundations and practical disciplines that are traditional in the established branches of engineering."[5] Different views of the nature of engineering led to different approaches to this goal, but in general they built on developments in systems software, extending programming languages and systems to encompass programming methodologies. Two main strains are of particular interest here: the use of programming environments to constrain the behavior of programmers and the extension of programming systems to encompass and ultimately to automate the entire software development cycle.

By the early 1970s, it seemed clear that, whatever the long-range prospects for automatic programming or at least for programming systems capable of representing large-scale computations in effective operational form, the development of software over the short term would rely on large numbers of programmers. Increasingly, programming systems came to be viewed in terms of disciplining programmers. Structured programming languages, enforced by diagnostic compilers, were aimed at constraining programmers to write clear, self-documenting, machine-independent programs. To place those programmers in a supportive environment, software engineers turned from mathematics and computer science to industrial engineering and project management for models of engineering practice. Arguing that, "Economical products of high quality are not possible (in most instances) when one instructs the programmer in good practice and merely hopes that he will make his invisible product according to those rules and standards," R. W. Bemer of GE spoke in 1968 of a "software factory" centered on the computer:

> It appears that we have few specific environments (factory facilities) for the economical production of programs. I contend that the production costs are affected far more adversely by the absence of such an environment than by the absence of any tools in the environment (e.g. writing a program in PL/1 is using a tool.)
>
> A factory supplies power, work space, shipping and receiving, labor distribution, and financial controls, etc. Thus a software factory should be a programming environment residing upon and controlled by a computer. Program construction, checkout and usage should be done entirely within this environment. Ideally it should be impossible to produce programs exterior to this environment.[6]

Much of the effort in software engineering during the 1970s and 1980s was directed toward the design and implementation of such environments, as the concept of the "software factory" took on a succession of forms. Computer-assisted software engineering (CASE) tools are perhaps the best example.

The Grail of Automatic Programming

While some software engineers thought of factories in terms of human workers organized toward efficient use of their labor, others looked to the automated factory first realized by Henry Ford's assembly line, where the product was built into the machines of production, leaving little or nothing to the skill of the worker. One aspect of that system attracted particular attention. Production by means of interchangeable parts was translated into such concepts as "mass-produced software components," modular programming, object-oriented programming, and reusable software. At the same time, in a manner similar to earlier work in compiler theory or indeed as an extension of it, research into formal methods of requirements analysis, specification, and design went hand in hand with the development of corresponding languages aimed at providing a continuous, automatic translation of a system from a description of its intended behavior to a working computer program. These efforts have so far met with only limited success. The production of programs remains in the hands of programmers.

NOTES

1. Herbert A. Simon, "The Corporation: Will It Be Managed By Machines?" published in 1961 in a volume of essays on *Management and Corporation: 1985*, ed. M. Anshen & G. L. Bach (McGraw-Hill, 1961); reprinted in *The World of the Computer,* ed. John Diebold (Random House, 1973), p. 154.

2. Maurice V. Wilkes, *Memoirs of a Computer Pioneer* (Cambridge, Mass.: MIT Press, 1985), p. 145.

3. H. Rutishauser wrote in 1967 ("Description of Algol 60," *Handbook for Automatic Computation* [Berlin: Springer]) that, "by 1954 the idea of using a computer for assisting the programmer had been seriously considered in Europe, but apparently none of these early algorithmic languages was ever put to actual use. The situation was quite different in the USA, where an assembly language epoch preceded the introduction of algorithmic languages. To some extent this may have diverted attention and energy from the latter, but on the other hand it helped to make automatic programming popular in the USA." (Quoted by Peter Naur in "The European Side of the Last Phase of the Development of Algol 60," *History of Programming Languages*, p. 93.)

4. Naur, "European Side," 95–96. In designing Algol 60, the members of the committee expressly barred discussions of implementation of the features of the language, albeit on the shared assumption that no one would propose a feature he did not know how to implement, at least in principle.

5. Peter Naur and Brian Randell, eds., *Software Engineering: Report on a Conference Sponsored by the NATO Science Committee, Garmisch, Germany 7th to 11th October 1968* (Brussels: NATO Scientific Affairs Division, January 1969), p. 13.

6. R. W. Bemer, "Position Paper for Panel Discussion [on] the Economics of Program Production," *Information Processing 68* (Amsterdam: North-Holland Publishing Company, 1969), II, p. 1626.

FOR FURTHER READING

Thomas M. Bergin and Richard G. Gibson, eds., *History of Programming Languages II* (New York: ACM Press; Reading, Mass.: Addison-Wesley Publishing Co., 1996).

Frederick P. Brooks, *The Mythical Man-Month: Essays on Software Engineering* (Reading, Mass.: Addison-Wesley Publishing Co., 1975; 3rd ed. 1995).

Paul W. Oman and Ted G. Lewis, eds., *Milestone in Software Evolution* (Los Alamitos, Calif.: IEEE Computer Society Press, 1990).

Saul Rosen, *Programming Systems and Languages* (New York: McGraw-Hill, 1967).

Norman Weizer, "A History of Operating Systems," *Datamation* (January 1981): 119–126.

Richard Wexelblat, ed., *History of Programming Languages* (New York: Academic Press, 1981).

8

A View from the Sixties: How the Software Industry Began

Luanne Johnson

You can't make any money selling software!" That was the conventional wisdom in the 1960s when software was either given away free by the computer manufacturers or written specifically and uniquely for each computer installation. Most executives in the computer industry didn't believe that there would ever be a significant market for software products.

But there were a few entrepreneurs who were convinced that you didn't have to write programs from scratch for each new computer installation. They believed that it was possible to write software that could be sold "off-the-shelf" over and over again to hundreds of customers.

They had some formidable obstacles to be overcome. There was the technical challenge of figuring out how to write computer programs that were robust enough and flexible enough to be used by many different customers—a difficult task given the limited memories of computers in the 1960s. But an even greater challenge was convincing customers that these programs were worth paying for when they were used to getting software for free from the computer manufacturers.

Unbundling

Today's conventional wisdom is that the software products industry began when IBM announced, on June 23, 1969, that it would begin pricing software separately from hardware beginning January 1, 1970. An article in *Computerworld* in June of 1989 headlined "Software industry born with IBM's unbundling" is a typical example of an attempt to identify unbundling as the singular event that made it possible to succeed as a software product company.

But the entrepreneurs who started their software companies in the 1960s will tell you that the industry was already well established by June of 1969. Larry Welke of International Computer Programs in Indianapolis, Indiana, began publishing a catalog of available software products in January 1967. In early 1971 he sponsored the first annual ICP Million Dollar Awards ceremony honoring 29 different software products that had sold over a million dollars each. The companies represented on this list of software vendors were formed well before IBM announced that it would begin charging for software, and that they had been enjoying success for several years is apparent from the sales volumes that entitled them to a place on the list.

There's no doubt, though, that IBM's unbundling helped to legitimize the concept of paying for software and was a great boon to the growing software industry. It represented a major change in the environment that was created by IBM, which totally dominated the computer market with a 70%+ market share throughout the 1960s and sold thousands of the System/360 series of computers introduced in 1964.

Customer Service

One of the major factors in IBM's success was its long-standing tradition of providing customer service at no charge. Its customers had virtually unlimited access to free classes in computer operations and programming for their employees and IBM systems engineers were assigned to each customer account to do whatever it took to get the customer's computer up and running. Theoretically, the systems engineers were supposed to be technical advisers to the customer's programmers but often "whatever it took" included writing the programs required to run their most urgently needed applications.

And IBM made all of the software in its growing library of programs available to its customers for free. Initially this library consisted primarily of general purpose programs such as language compilers or utility programs such as sorts. Over time, however, many of the programs written by IBM systems engineers "in the field" for their customers' applications became added to the library of programs available to all IBM users for free.

All of these support services were considered by IBM to be part of its marketing expense, and the cost of providing them was included in the cost of the hardware. It was a very successful marketing strategy in spite of the fact that bundling the cost of all these extra services into the hardware costs pushed the price up. The sense of having IBM's vast resources available to them at no additional charge gave its customers confidence that they were going to be able to get whatever they needed to make their computers work. And it created an environment where customers did not expect to have to pay for software.

It was also common practice for computer users to share program code they had written with other users. This practice was perpetuated through the associations SHARE and GUIDE, which were formed by IBM customers in the mid-1950s for the purpose of sharing what they learned in the process of installing and programming their computers. The company assisted its customers in this process of sharing programs among themselves by maintaining the library of programs contributed by SHARE and GUIDE members and including them in a catalog of programs available free of charge to all IBM customers.

Software Services

The success of IBM and the other computer manufacturers in selling computers during the late 1950s and early 1960s created a huge demand for people with even a couple of years of programming experience. Hundreds of programmers with an entrepreneurial bent quit their jobs to form new companies so that they could sell their software development services at a premium—often back to the companies that had paid them while they had learned their skills in the first place.

The first software services firm was Computer Usage Corporation (CUC), founded in 1955 by John W. Sheldon and Elmer C. Kubie, who left the scientific programming division of IBM in order to form the company. It was soon joined by other software services firms, such as Computer Sciences Corporation (CSC), the Planning Research Corporation (PRC), California Analysis Centers, Inc. (CACI), Management Science America (MSA), and Informatics and Applied Data Research (ADR). It's estimated that by 1965, there were 40–50 major software services firms in the United States, a handful of whom had annual revenues of $10–$100 million. In addition, there were probably a couple of thousand very small firms, consisting of one or two programmers.

The software services industry was the incubator for the software products industry. It was not unusual for these firms to reuse program code that had been developed for one client in developing an application for another client, modifying it as needed for the new application. Because the practice of reusing code was so common, there are a number of firms that have claimed that they developed the first software product, meaning that they developed a program that was used by several different customers without extensive modifications.

However, most of these firms remained focused on selling services and didn't make selling software products a priority. If we define the first true software product as one that not only was sold off-the-shelf to many users over and over again but also resulted in a company that was organized around the development and marketing of software products, the answer is easy. The product was AUTOFLOW, introduced in 1965; the company was Applied Data Research.

Applied Data Research

Applied Data Research was founded in Princeton, New Jersey, in 1959, by seven programmers (Sherman Blumenthal, Martin A. Goetz, Elwood Kaufman, Dave McFadden, Bernard Riskin, Robert Wickenden, and Steven Wright) who had worked at Sperry-Rand, manufacturer of the UNIVAC computer. Their plan was to sell their services as experienced programmers to write the software needed by Sperry-Rand and other computer manufacturers.

In 1964, RCA was an up-and-coming computer manufacturer and one of ADR's premier customers. It approached ADR about writing a flow-charting program that would visually represent the logical flow of instructions in a program. Consistent with the practice of all the major computer manufacturers at that time, the program would be provided to its customers at no cost. Applied Data Research designed and wrote a program that would sequentially read through all the commands in a program and produce such a flowchart and offered it to RCA for $25,000, but the RCA executives decided that they weren't interested at that price.

Martin A. (Marty) Goetz was the member of ADR's management team who had responsibility for the project. The company had about $10,000 invested in the program, so Goetz decided to try to license it to RCA's customer base of about a hundred RCA 501 users with the hope of recouping the investment. He called the program AUTOFLOW, priced it at $2,400, and prepared some descriptive marketing material that they sent to all 100 users. He got two takers.

Given that the conventional wisdom at the time was that you can't make any money selling software, Goetz could have decided that he had proved that point. But Goetz is a stubborn man. Still looking to recoup ADR's investment, he noted that, although there were only about a hundred companies using the RCA 501, there were thousands using IBM 1401 computers. He decided that AUTOFLOW could be a financial success in the IBM market.

That meant, however, that AUTOFLOW, which was designed to process programs written in RCA's Assembler language, had to be completely rewritten to handle programs written in Autocoder, the favored language of IBM 1401 programmers. Ten months later a new version of AUTOFLOW, which would produce flowcharts for Autocoder programs, was completed and ADR began trying to sell it in the IBM marketplace.

This time there was a lot more interest, but still not many buyers. AUTOFLOW had one serious design limitation. It required that the programmer add a one-digit code to each instruction in the program to tell AUTOFLOW what type of instruction it was—whether it accessed a file, or performed a calculation, or tested a condition for branching to another instruction. This was not a serious inconvenience when a new program was written from scratch. But the IBM 1401 computers had been around for several years and a typical customer had hundreds of programs sitting around that had already been written. Those were the programs for which they wanted to prepare flowcharts and AUTOFLOW couldn't do it.

Flowcharting as a programming technique was developed in the late 1940s before the invention of symbolic programming languages. Early computer programs written in machine language required that the programmer keep track of the actual machine address where an instruction was stored in memory. If a new instruction was inserted, it changed the addresses of all the instructions from that point forward in the program, which required rewriting all the succeeding instructions. Flowcharting allowed a programmer to lay out a graphical representation of the logical flow of the program and make sure that all the steps were included before assigning the addresses to each step.

By the mid-1960s, the vast majority of programmers were no longer writing in machine language and they were no longer required to keep track of the actual machine addresses for the program instructions. But the practice of drawing a flowchart before beginning to write a program was well-entrenched and programmers were still trained to begin the programming process with a flowchart.

In practice, however, hardly anyone ever drew the flowcharts because hardly anyone ever wrote a program from scratch. It was much easier to take a similar, existing program, make a duplicate of the deck of punched cards on which the source code was stored, and then add and delete cards as needed to create the new program. The flowchart, if there was one, of the original program, hand-drawn on large sheets of specially designed paper provided by IBM, was much more difficult to modify, so it never got changed. But preparing and maintaining a flowchart on file for every operational program continued to be the official policy in most data processing departments.

What ADR learned when they tried to sell AUTOFLOW to IBM 1401 customers was that people were mildly interested in a program that helped them create flowcharts for programs they were writing from scratch, but were desperate for a way to flowchart all the programs they already had that had never been flowcharted in the first place.

So it was back to the drawing board once again for AUTOFLOW. This time the program was designed to actually parse the instructions in the Autocoder program to determine what symbol should be drawn on the flowchart instead of looking for a special code. Now the source code for any existing Autocoder program could be fed into AUTOFLOW and a flowchart of the program's logical sequence would be printed out. If the program was changed, it simply had to be run through AUTOFLOW again and an updated flowchart would print out. This time ADR had something that customers really wanted—and ran smack up against IBM's policy of giving away programs for free.

AUTOFLOW sold quite well. As a matter of fact, considering that in 1965 no one had ever sold a significant number of copies of a software product for a price, it sold remarkably well. But what should have been a natural market of thousands of potential customers was severely constrained by the belief on the part of those customers that the product that ADR was selling for $2,400 could be gotten for free from IBM.

A flowcharting program called Flowcharter had been developed by one of IBM's systems engineers and was available to all IBM customers for free. But it wasn't automatic. It didn't prepare the flowchart by parsing the program code as AUTOFLOW did; it didn't use the program code at all. Instead it required that the programmer prepare a separate set of coding sheets that would be used by the program to draw the flowchart. It reduced the process of preparing the flowchart to a kind of shorthand that the Flowcharter program expanded into a flowchart. But it didn't replace the flowcharting step completely as AUTOFLOW did.

Customers were, of course, aware that AUTOFLOW provided a functionality that didn't exist in Flowcharter. But they were also convinced that it was only a matter of time before IBM would produce a similar product and that they'd get it for free. Over and over again, as a result of a sales presentation on AUTOFLOW, the potential customer would call his IBM account representative and ask when they were going to upgrade their program to do what AUTOFLOW did. The company didn't respond to every customer request for upgrades to its free programs, but requests that came from a lot of IBM customers were difficult to ignore. So the more aggressively that ADR sold AUTOFLOW, the greater the likelihood became that IBM would produce a product with comparable functionality and offer it for free, effectively putting ADR out of the software products business.

Goetz took defensive action. He applied for a patent on AUTOFLOW and served notice on IBM that they might be violating ADR's patent application if they produced an automatic flowcharting program. As a result, he became the first-ever recipient of a patent on software, issued in 1968, a clear turning-point in the recognition of software as a product, not a service.

Goetz also faced the possibility that potential customers would get a copy of AUTOFLOW from another customer rather than paying ADR for it, since sharing programs among users was a customary and accepted practice. He consulted with Mort Jacobs, the attorney who had prepared the patent application, and they decided that the solution to the problem was to lease the software to the customer rather than sell it. Legally, when a product is sold, its ownership transfers to the customer who is free to do with it as he or she pleases. A customer who buys a car from General Motors is free to resell the car to anyone else under any terms he or she wishes. This doesn't represent a threat to companies that produce products with a high manufacturing cost per copy but is a serious problem for software companies where reproduction of their product is extremely easy and inexpensive.

The agreement that ADR's customers signed was not a sales agreement but an an equipment lease agreement (with the software defined as a piece of equipment) which gave the customer the right to use the software for the term of the agreement (usually three years) but, like a piece of equipment leased for a period and then returned to the leasing company, the customer never actually owned the software. This didn't make it any more difficult for a programmer to make and distribute copies of the software but at least it gave ADR a basis for taking legal action against someone who did so.

With the success of IBM's sales of System/360, ADR made the decision to rewrite AUTOFLOW yet again, this time to process programs written in the three programming languages most favored by System/360 users: 360 Assembly Language, FORTRAN, and COBOL. By 1970, ADR had several thousand customers using AUTOFLOW and 30 sales offices throughout the United States and Europe.

Over the next several years, ADR developed several other software products that could be sold into its established customer base, and by the late 1970s it was one of the top five software products companies in the world. Although ADR continued throughout its life to have a small division providing programming services, by the mid-1970s less than 10% of ADR's revenues were from services; ADR had, to all intents and purposes, transformed itself from a software services company into a software products company.

By 1984, ADR had nearly 20,000 copies of its software products installed in 9,000 customer sites; in 1985, it was sold to Ameritech for $200 million.

Conclusion

In December of 1968, in an attempt to prevent a U.S. government antitrust suit, IBM announced that it was going to change its pricing policies on software. The announcement stated that a task force was being established to review the current policies and recommend new ones, and that the new policies would be announced in June, 1969. But the attempt to avoid the antitrust suit was unsuccessful.

On January 17, 1969, the last day of the Johnson Administration, Attorney General Ramsey Clark directed the Justice Department to file an antitrust suit against IBM, leaving the suit to be pursued by the incoming Nixon administration. The complaint, which focused on IBM's dominance in hardware, also addressed the software industry's concerns that IBM had inhibited the growth of the software products industry through its bundling of hardware and software. The suit dragged on for over 18 years before it was finally withdrawn.

The outcome of the efforts of the IBM task force that labored through the early months of 1969 was at least a partial unbundling of software from hardware. On June 30, 1969, IBM announced that it would reduce the price of its hardware leases by 3% and would begin to charge separately for customer training, for system engineering services, and for some software beginning on January 1, 1970.

The impact of the unbundling decision on IBM and on the hardware and software industries has been explored at length in numerous books, articles and papers. It was certainly an important event in the history of the software industry, but it is also clear that a number of software companies had been able to compete very effectively even against the free software from IBM. The other factors affecting the creation of the software industry will remain obscure until the early years of the mainframe software industry are researched and explored with the same interest and enthusiasm that is given to the PC software industry. It was an exciting, fertile era of entrepreneurial zest and imaginative risk-taking. It deserves its share of the historical spotlight.

ACKNOWLEDGMENTS

Portions reprinted, with permission, from *IEEE Annals of the History of Computing* 20/1 (1998): 36–42. © 1998 IEEE.

NOTES

Detailed references to the interviews and published sources used for this chapter can be found in the original article of the same title in *IEEE Annals of the History of Computing* 20/1 (1998): 36–42. In addition to those references, material pertaining to this chapter can be found in R.L. Forman, *Fulfilling the Computer's Promise: The History of Informatics, 1962–1968* (Woodland Hills, Calif.: Informatics, 1985); E.W. Pugh, *Building IBM: Shaping an Industry and Its Technology* (Cambridge, Mass.: MIT Press, 1995); S. Gibson, "Software Industry Born with IBM Unbundling," *Computerworld* (19 June 1989); E.C. Kubie, "Recollections of the First Software Company," *IEEE Annals of the History of Computing* 16/2 (1994):65–71; and in the author's interviews of Walter F. Bauer, Wilfred J. Dixon, Martin A. Goetz, and others (interviews in author's possession).

FOR FURTHER READING

Walter F. Bauer, "Informatics: An Early Software Company," *IEEE Annals of the History of Computing* 18/2 (1996): 70–76.

Martin Campbell-Kelly, "Development and Structure of the International Software Industry, 1950–1990," *Business and Economic History* 24/2 (Winter 1995): 84–85.

Martin Campbell-Kelly and William Aspray, *Computer: A History of the Information Machine* (New York: Basic Books, 1996), pp. 181–205 and 259–282.

Robert L. Glass, *In the Beginning: Recollections of Software Pioneers* (Los Alamitos, Calif.: IEEE Computer Society, 1998).

Jean E. Sammet, *Programming Languages: History and Fundamentals* (Englewood Cliffs, N.J.: Prentice-Hall, 1969).

9

Personal Computer Software

Paul Ceruzzi

An understanding of the history of software for the personal computer must begin with an understanding of the social phenomena of the its invention, and its spread from its hobbyist roots into the mainstream. Like the commercial computer of 1951, the personal computer was not supposed to happen. Those who knew the most about hardware and software thought they knew where computing was headed in the 1970s. But none of them thought that the Altair—the computer that started the PC phenomenon—was on that road.

It was not that people were opposed to bringing computing out of its restricted-access place in the computing center. The thrust of many timesharing projects of the early 1970s was to do just that. Nor was it a secret that chip density was moving at a pace that would make a computer-on-a-chip technically feasible. The UNIVAC I had on the order of 32,000 components, of which 5,500 were vacuum tubes. That number of components was already being fabricated on a few, select chips by the mid-1970s.

Still, none of this explains the appearance of the Altair on the cover of the January 1975 issue of *Popular Electronics,* or the firestorm of interest that the $400 kits generated. Nor does it explain the chain of events that led to Microsoft's dominance over PC software, and the Intel 8080 architecture's dominance over PC hardware, which continues to this very day.

Mark Twain once said, "In the past nothing ever happened at the right time, in the right place, or in the right way. It is the job of the historian to remedy that deficiency." Many people have taken Twain at his word and used the benefit of hindsight to reconstitute events, quite often not in the way that they happened. I make a modest effort here to place early developments in PC software into an accurate order that somehow also makes sense.

I leave the larger story of the personal computer's invention to other accounts, but it is worth mentioning a number of concerns that kept manufacturers skeptical of personal computing in general. Some raised the objection that most owners of personal computers would lack the skills needed to maintain them. There was the concern that users lacked the skills to fit their computers into a practical system that did useful work, a skill known in the mainframe world as "systems engineering." And there was the objection that personal computers, with their small internal memories and unreliable or nonexistent mass storage devices, would be useless for applications that required handling even modest amounts of data: applications that were routine in the mainframe and even minicomputer world. Finally, there was the objection that PC users would have to write their own software, something that professional programmers struggled to do with larger machines. Given these objections, it seemed that a line of personal computers descended from the Altair would be a dead-end.

As it turned out, each of these objections was met in turn. Although the Altair itself was not very reliable, later "clones" of it, and other personal computers, were. Increased chip density, which meant fewer interconnections outside of the chip, led to increased reliability. Integrating the computer into a practical system was indeed a serious concern—using a computer was not a passive activity like watching television. That need was filled by a sophisticated, and largely free, support structure that soon emerged. User groups had been around since SHARE in the 1950s, but PC user clubs had a distinctive and very open flavor. While the Home Brew Computer Club of northern California has been elevated to mythical proportions, there is a lot of truth behind its myth. It and many less well known user clubs published newsletters, provided hotlines, and offered a generally supportive atmosphere that welcomed newcomers, no matter how inexperienced they were. The objection that computers needed large data storage was finessed by users who concentrated on applications that did not process large amounts of data. Foremost among the early uses of the personal computer were games, which required no major data sets. Like other new technologies, the personal computer found new uses rather than performing old tasks such as crunching large volumes of numbers.

The most serious objection was that people would have to learn to program their own computers. Computers, however powerful, could do nothing by themselves. Without software, the machine would sit idly with hardly a blinking light. That objection was eventually met by the development of packaged applications, but before that there was a genuine need for users to write their own programs. And it was not easy. The following narrative traces the steps that PC enthusiasts took to meet this objection.

Programming the Microprocessor

To preface this story, we consider first how the issue of software appeared to companies like Intel, which designed and built microprocessors—the chips that incorporated all the processing functions of a computer on one or two pieces of silicon. It was significant that Intel, Texas Instruments, and the other semiconductor companies were just that: semiconductor, not computer companies. They saw the total market for a given computer along the lines of, say, Digital Equipment Corporation's PDP-8, which was the most popular machine that was being produced at the time. According to Digital Equipment's own corporate history, "More than 1,200 'classic' PDP-8 systems were manufactured, and a total of 40,000 PDP-8 systems ultimately produced." Those numbers were very large for a computer company, but very small for a semiconductor firm. For these latter companies, that sales volume was too small for the tooling and design costs, so that neither the hardware nor the software of a personal computer was within their immediate plans.

Therefore these companies thought of the microprocessor not as the nucleus of a general purpose computer but as a versatile controller, which they could embed into other machines: gas pumps, point-of-sale terminals, numerically controlled machine tools, and so on. That was where the volume was. Incidentally, that is still how microprocessor companies recoup the development costs—as they sell the newest version of a chip for the latest personal computer (e.g., Pentium III), they cut the price of the ones just made "obsolete" and sell them in tremendous volume in embedded applications. The 8-bit Zilog Z-80, for example, may still be one of the world's best-selling processors, more than a decade after its introduction, even though personal computers that use it are no longer made.

For these machines the programming is done once, compiled into machine language, burned into a read-only memory (ROM) chip, and embedded deep into the machine, where no one would have access to it except in a few precisely defined ways. That kind of programming was done on a mainframe, using all the tools and high-level languages available on a mainframe installation. The mainframe then "cross-compiled" or "cross-assembled" the program: it generated machine code for the microprocessor's (not its own) instruction set, and this code was then burned into a ROM.

The need to have access to a mainframe made this process expensive. To save costs, some semiconductor companies built and offered to its customers a small computer, somewhat like the PDP-8 minicomputer, specially tailored to execute the instructions of the microprocessor they hoped to sell in volume. An engineer could use this machine to develop, debug, and test processor code quickly, before making the commitment to putting the code into a ROM. One mid-1970s example was Rockwell's "Assemulator" built to emulate its 4-bit microprocessor.

Finally, the semiconductor company might build a dedicated computer using the actual microprocessor itself. These machines could not offer the sophisticated programming and debugging tools of a mainframe, but they cost less. They were therefore useful as a developmental tool for the myriad of embedded systems being designed by specialized engineering firms both large and small. With hindsight, we now know these development systems were among the first microprocessor-based computers ever built. The Intellec-4 and Intellec-8, built by Intel, fit this category. But neither the chip companies nor their customers saw these as general purpose computers. Nor did the manufacturers think of themselves as being in the computer business. Gary Kildall, an instructor at the Naval Postgraduate School in Monterey, California, was working with these Intel systems to develop applications for Navy divers. In a report of his work, he expressed the common view, that "the manufacturer's development systems are generally in appropriate [sic] as end-user products."

In any case, programming a microprocessor implied using a high-level language, and then compiling the code into instructions that the micro-processor could recognize. In 1973, Kildall developed "PL/M," a cross-compiler based on IBM's PL/I language developed for the System/360. PL/M programs retained the look and structure of the mainframe culture from which it descended, including the slash–asterisk (/*) used to denote comments. Initial versions ran on IBM System/360 mainframes. Output was an intermediate code that was loaded, by paper tape, onto a small development system, which in turn produced machine code that went into a ROM. Variations of this activity still go on at thousands of locations around the world today. But that is not what we think of when we think of PC software. That story has different roots, beginning with the development of a programming language at Dartmouth College in 1964.

BASIC

For personal computers, the initial concern was to find a suitable high-level programming language. It had to fit into the severe memory constraints of the machine, be easy to learn, yet powerful enough to develop programs that went beyond simple teaching or demonstrations. The PC world converged quickly on BASIC as that language—so quickly that it is often overlooked how many other languages or systems were contenders, at least before 1977. But BASIC it was.

The BASIC that emerged as the standard for personal computers differed in fundamental ways from the language developed by John Kemeny and Thomas Kurtz at Dartmouth College a decade earlier. The primary reason was the personal computer's severe memory constraints, in contrast to the situation at Dartmouth, where BASIC ran on a large General Electric mainframe. Other factors played a role as well, including the substantial support network that grew up among early PC users. Kemeny and Kurtz designed a language that would be easy to learn, especially by undergraduates at a school where liberal-arts majors outnumbered those studying engineering or the physical sciences. Many hobbyists who bought the first personal computers were likewise not engineers or scientists, but they had a support network of fellow hobbyists to draw on when they needed help. Thus the BASIC programming language for the personal computer could sacrifice some of that ease of learning to make it fit into a smaller computer. Thus, although BASIC for the personal computer was a language that in many ways was closer to assembler or even machine code than the Dartmouth version, it was still one that users found easy enough to learn because of the social network that emerged to support it.

Many versions of this language appeared between 1975 and 1977, but the one written by Bill Gates, Paul Allen, and Monte Davidoff for the Altair emerged as the first among them. A comparison of the features, background, and history of all the PC languages that emerged between 1975 and 1977 will be a topic for future research. What follows is a brief look at nature and origin of those features of Microsoft BASIC that set it apart.

BASIC was developed by Kemeny and Kurtz for a timesharing system, intended for use by undergraduates at a liberal arts college. That history has been well told in the first History of Programming Languages Conference proceedings. Dartmouth BASIC was not the immediate ancestor of the BASIC that came to dominate personal computers. The immediate ancestor of Microsoft BASIC was a version developed by the

Digital Equipment Corporation (DEC) for their "Resource Sharing Time Sharing" (RSTS-11) system, offered with a PDP-11/20 beginning in 1971 and subsequently extended to other models. The PDP-11 (and especially the PDP-11/20) was a 16-bit minicomputer with only a fraction of the memory of the General Electric mainframe used at Dartmouth. It therefore required a version of BASIC quite different from that of the GE mainframe, or any other computer used for a commercial timesharing system.

The RSTS-11 had few of the features, such as memory protection, that most thought a timesharing system had to have. Engineers at DEC wrote a version of BASIC that served double duty: in addition to being a language for users to program their own applications with, it also handled system calls and general housekeeping that allowed the resources of the computer to be shared in the first place. In order to do that, the language needed a way for privileged users to call system functions, to look at the contents of specific locations in memory, and directly deposit bytes of data into specific memory locations. In the BASIC that was shipped with RSTS-11 these were called "SYS," "PEEK," and "POKE" respectively.

According to legend, Gates and Allen decided to write a BASIC compiler for the Altair immediately upon seeing the announcement for the kit. In a newsletter sent out to Altair customers, they said a version requiring 4K bytes of memory would be available by June 1975, barely six months after the *Popular Electronics* article and at a time when very few real machines actually existed. More powerful versions would come later. They did in fact produce a version for the Altair. Like most others at the time who developed microprocessor software, they used a large timeshared mainframe to do their development work, rather than the 8080 itself (which they did not have access to anyway). As a Harvard student, Gates had access to a PDP-10 installed at Harvard's Computation Laboratory. It was on that PDP-10 where BASIC for the Altair was written.

From RSTS-11 they borrowed the PEEK and POKE commands; from another DEC system they borrowed a command called "USR" (User Service Routine), which allowed a programmer to drop out of BASIC and transfer program control to subroutines written in machine language. Kemeny and Kurtz believed that, for mainly pedagogic reasons, certain tenets of BASIC were sacred: the "LET" command to indicate assignment, for example; also the requirement that each statement be on a separate line with its own line number. Altair BASIC, later called Microsoft BASIC, broke both conventions along with many others too numerous to mention. In general, Microsoft BASIC sacrificed readability and clarity for increased capability and the economical use of memory. The result was something genuinely useful for the 8080-based personal computer that had appeared on the market.

Based mainly on the success of that language, Microsoft, the company Gates and Allen founded in Albuquerque, was able to break away from its connection with MITS (the Albuquerque company that made the Altair computer) and move to Seattle in 1978 (see figure 9.1). Microsoft offered or promised compilers for other languages, but none had an impact on BASIC. It remained central to the development of PC software for a decade, until "Turbo Pascal" from Borland unseated it in 1983.

CP/M and Disk Storage

Second only to the emergence of BASIC for personal computers was the emergence of a suitable operating system. That story is also dominated by Microsoft. One can also say that after Microsoft's move to Seattle, operating systems defined Microsoft's role in the PC software industry just as BASIC defined it before.

Figure 9.1. Microsoft employees, ca. 1978. This photograph depicts Microsoft as it was preparing to move from Albuquerque, New Mexico, where it was founded, to the Seattle, Washington area. Its founders, Bill Gates and Paul Allen, are at the lower left and lower right, respectively. At this time Microsoft was still primarily a supplier of BASIC and other programming languages for personal computers. Courtesy of Microsoft Corporation. © 1978 Microsoft Corporation.

Like the story of BASIC, the development of a PC operating system owes a lot to prior work done by DEC. Some of the work was even done at the project at MIT's Lincoln Labs that led to the founding of DEC. The idea there was to develop a method of computer access that would later be known as interactive and conversational. Some of the specific advances had to do with providing access to files that were stored on magnetic tapes, drums, and disks, the ease of which was a crucial foundation for interactive systems.

Meanwhile, many of the earliest personal computers used ordinary cassette tape as their mass storage devices, where data was encoded as audio tones. This convention was developed by a group of hobbyists and early PC manufacturers who met in Kansas City in 1975. However, by the time this "Kansas City Standard" emerged it was already clear to many users that they needed the random access storage of floppy disks. Gary Kildall (see figure 9.2), whom we have already met as the author of Intel's PL/M, wrote a small control program for a floppy-disk drive that he attached to one of the Intel development kits mentioned above. In what proved to be an understatement, he remarked in an interview published in the book *Programmers at Work* (Redmond, Wa., 1986, p. 61) that "It turned out that the operating system, which was called CP/M for Control Program for Micros, was useful, too...." He began selling CP/M commercially, and sales were so good that in 1976 he quit his job at the Naval Postgraduate School and founded a company called Intergalactic Digital Research (later shortened to Digital Research).

Figure 9.2. Gary Kildall, ca. 1978. Kildall's CP/M operating system helped establish a commercial software industry for personal computers. In this photograph he is sitting in front of a DEC minicomputer. Courtesy of Kristen Kildall.

In his first published description of CP/M, Kildall stated that it descended from PL/M, which again was a variant of PL/I. But a look at CP/M's commands shows a different ancestry. Among the programs supplied with CP/M were "TECO" (Text Editor and COrrector), "DDT" (Dynamic Debugging Tool, also known as DEC Debugging Tape), and "PIP" (Peripheral Interchange Program). These were found among the commands offered with DEC's operating systems. The DDT program was originally written by Thomas J. Stockham for the TX-0, an experimental transistorized computer built at Lincoln Labs by members of Project Whirlwind, and was running by 1957 (there it was originally called "FLIT" [Flexowriter Interrogation Tape]). It was rewritten for the PDP-1, DEC's first computer, and was adapted to many of DEC's early systems, especially the PDP-10. Members of the MIT Tech Model Railroad Club are said to have done much of the conversion work. The TECO program was written by Dan Murphy originally for a PDP-1 installed at MIT around 1963.

The PIP program was flexible and allowed files to be moved in a variety of different ways; it was written for the PDP-6 by Harrison "Dit" Morse and later modified by Dave Gross. Both were DEC employees. It was originally called "Atlatl," which an unabridged dictionary says is a device that spear-throwers used to leverage the strength of their arms and thereby increase the spear's range.

This journey into the arcane world of minicomputer engineers, MIT Model Railroad Club members, and Lincoln Lab scientists is not only a pleasant but also a necessary diversion from the main theme of PC operating systems. It shows how the foundations of PC system software had deep roots in the very earliest days of electronic computers, even while companies like Microsoft saw themselves as breaking away from the social milieu of those years.

Kildall found himself busy adapting CP/M for a variety of 8080-based personal computers. In 1977 he decided to separate out those aspects of the language that were specific to one Altair clone—the IMSAI—and put it into a section of code he called the "BIOS" (Basic Input/Output System). This paved the way for CP/M to become a de facto standard for nearly all 8080-based personal computers. That in turn opened up the market for commercial, commodity software.

Commodity software was what really set personal computing apart from its ancestors. But before I turn to this account, I will comment briefly on the critical—and now legendary—shift from CP/M to MS-DOS (Microsoft Disk Operating System), which came with the arrival of the IBM personal computer in 1981.

In August 1980, IBM representatives met with people at Digital Research to explore the option of using a 16-bit version of CP/M for their new personal computer. This meeting ended without any agreement, and when their computer was unveiled a year later, it came with "PC-DOS," which IBM obtained from Microsoft. That story has been told many times—even reconstructed, inaccurately I believe, on national television in an episode of a series aired by PBS.

What is known is that PC-DOS (which was sold for PC clones as MS-DOS) was based on a system called "86-DOS," which Microsoft obtained from a small company called Seattle Computer Products. Tim Paterson wrote most of 86-DOS, he has said, because he did not want to wait for the operating system Digital Research promised for the new Intel 16-bit chip. In some descriptions of 86-DOS it is called "Q-DOS" (Quick and Dirty Operating System). It is similar to CP/M in many ways: the commands "type," "rename," and "erase" are found in both, and they work the same way (except for their reversed syntax for source and destination). But there are differences, too. All of the old DEC commands, some of which were in operating systems since 1957, were gone. That may be the strongest evidence supporting Tim Paterson's claim that he did not simply rewrite CP/M for the new Intel chip.

No one before him produced a piece of software with quite the impact his had. Paterson freely acknowledges that he was influenced by lots of sources—just like every software developer before him. The DEC engineers and former MIT students certainly borrowed freely from one another, and those whom I have interviewed have never indicated that this was anything unusual or wrong. Neither did they express anything but pride in the fact that their work proved to be so influential on the development of personal computing. This may have been natural for those who belonged to DEC, since DEC was a computer company that developed software in order to get more people to buy computers.

Paterson also claims that he never saw any CP/M source code. Like Gates and Allen before him, Paterson did not work on an 8086 system but from an Intel specification sheet for the new chip. Paterson wrote 86-DOS in 8080 assembly language on a Z-80 computer, which he cross-compiled to produce 8086 object code. He recalls spending about two man-months on the original operating system, which generated about 6 K of object code.

Although Digital Research continued to prosper, Kildall became embittered by what he felt was a theft by Paterson. Worse, he felt outmaneuvered by Gates. He became depressed, began drinking heavily, and died in July 1994. The exact cause of death was never determined. By then MS-DOS laid the foundation for the commercial PC software industry by providing a standard operating system for most personal computers.

Applications

Historian Martin Campbell-Kelly has written an excellent survey of the economics and background for early software applications (see Further Reading below). I wish only to emphasize the "big three": word processing, spreadsheets, and databases. Each appeared relatively early and continue to dominate the market. Visicalc first appeared in 1979. It was soon enhanced by "Visiplot," a graphics enhancement that was written by Mitch Kapor, who later produced Lotus 1-2-3. Early versions of Word Star (originally Word Master) and dBase II (known originally as "Vulcan," which the Jet Propulsion Laboratory developed for the U.S. space program) also appeared the same year. All of these were developed for 8-bit hardware. The three programs were the PC equivalents of FORTRAN and COBOL during the mainframe era. They were universally popular and long-lasting in spite of numerous efforts to develop extensions, improvements, and new paradigms for PC usage.

Parallel to the big three was the development of games, whose influence on personal computing was far greater than their subject matter might suggest. "Black Jack," for example, was one of the first programs written in Gates's and Allen's BASIC. Bruce Artwick's Flight Simulator appeared in 1980. Originally written for the Apple II, it was purchased by Microsoft and continues to be a top-selling program under Windows. Campbell-Kelly has pointed out how the user interface is a much more critical issue for PC software than for mainframe software. This issue was first encountered in the development of interactive games. Games continue to be a major market for PC software, and its products spill over into the educational software market.

The only other major addition to that triumvirate has been communications software, either for local networks or for the Internet. Here the story of PC software merges with the "mainstream" history of computing, with its emphasis on UNIX, Ethernet, the VAX, and the ARPANET. Networking came late to personal computing. Part of the reason was the severe limits of early microprocessors, even with 16-bit chips like the Intel 8088. An equally important reason was the early culture of PC users. Personal computers were pushed into the world by people who wanted to escape the tyranny of the computer center. As personal computing entered into the office and into the respectability of the mainstream world, it only grudgingly abandoned its early cultural roots. A number of networking schemes were floated almost as soon as the 16-bit computers appeared. Novell's Netware, introduced in 1983, emerged to dominate the field.

Conclusion

One thread that runs through this brief survey of PC software is how deeply its roots extend into earlier systems. Few programs were developed on the microprocessor-based systems for which they were sold. Microsoft BASIC was initially developed on a PDP-10, as was the original version of the "Adventure" game. Visicalc was developed on a Honeywell Multics system. Its creators, Daniel Bricklin and Robert Frankston, were members of the legendary Project MAC at MIT, where so much research on interactive computing was done (the acronym had a dual meaning: "Machine-Aided Cognition," and "Multiple-Access Computer"). The CP/M grew out of work on IBM mainframes and PL/I. Many early word processors grew out of dedicated word processing machines like those offered by CPT and NBI, and from word processing software first written for minicomputers—such as "DecMate" written for Digital's PDP-8 (a system authored in part by Dan Bricklin). This fits well with the observation about the technical roots of the microprocessor and the personal computer itself. To return to Mark Twain's observation about history, the story of the development of PC software is paradoxical. The examples described above show that it was a logical progression from work that had been going on in the minicomputer and even mainframe culture. Yet one cannot escape the notion of the emergence of PC software, and of Microsoft, as a revolutionary and illogical break with computing's past.

FOR FURTHER READING

Martin Campbell-Kelly, "Global Perspectives on the Software Industry, 1950–1990," *Business and Economic History*, 24/2 (Winter 1995): 73–110.

Paul Ceruzzi, *A History of Modern Computing* (Cambridge, Mass.: MIT Press, 1998).

Stephen Manes and Paul Andrews, *Gates: How Microsoft's Mogul Reinvented an Industry—and Made Himself the Richest Man in America* (New York: Doubleday, 1993).

Forrest Mims, III, *Siliconnections* (New York: McGraw-Hill, 1986).

10

Computer Networks

Janet Abbate

Computer networks are perhaps the most significant comput-ing development of the late 20th century. Networks have radically changed both the number and type of people who have access to computers and the kinds of activities that computers are used to support. This chapter surveys four topics in the history of computer networks: early data communications experiments, the ARPANET and Internet, local-area networks, and the World Wide Web.

Early Data Communications

The history of networking is tied up with the history of interactive computer systems, since the main motive for building networks has been to allow interaction with remote computers. An early example is the U.S. Defense Department's Project SAGE, a computerized early-warning system built in the 1950s to detect missile attacks. Each SAGE center had an IBM mainframe that received data through telephone lines from dozens of radar installations and military bases. One of the technologies developed for SAGE was the modem, which converts digital computer data into analog signals that can be sent over the telephone network. Modems became available for general use in 1958, and by 1968 annual modem sales in the United States had reached 85,000.

Modems solved the basic data communications problem of connecting a terminal to a computer over a long distance, but they introduced new difficulties. Long-distance communications could be quite costly for the computer owner, and some machines had difficulty handling a large number of connections. New peripheral devices were invented to help rationalize the terminal handling. These included concentrators, which collect the input from many terminals and send it over a single link to the computer, and front ends, which are small computers that stand between the mainframe and the communications link and handle the data traffic, leaving the main computer free to do other tasks.

A number of experimental systems in the late 1950s and early 1960s connected decentralized terminals with computer centers at universities, research laboratories, and businesses. By the mid-1960s, commercial timesharing services were also developing their own data networks to give their customers low-cost access to their computers. A number of data intensive industries, such as airlines and stock exchanges, built cooperative networks in the 1960s, which allowed a number of firms to share a common pool of information. In the early 1960s, American Airlines and IBM created the SABRE online reservation system (based on IBM's work on SAGE), which connected 2,000 terminals across the United States to a central computer. Following this, an international cooperative of 175 airlines called SITA (Société Internationale de Télécommunications Aéronautiques) built a network connecting nine centers in Amsterdam, Brussels, Frankfurt, Hong Kong, London, Madrid, New York, Paris, and Rome. In 1970 a network for stock quotations, the National Association of Securities Dealers Automated Quotation System (NASDAQ) was constructed, and by 1975, NASDAQ had several computer centers and 1,700 terminals attached.

All of the networks just mentioned were designed to connect terminals to a computer center. There were also some experiments in the 1960s on exchanging data between computers. Because of the difficulty at this time of connecting computers of different manufacturers, these networks were restricted to linking computers from the same product line, generally IBM 360s. One such project was the 1966 Triangle Universities Computation Center Network, a cooperative project of Duke University, North Carolina State University, and the University of North Carolina; a similar network connected IBM 360 computers at Carnegie-Mellon and Princeton. Universities built these networks to even out the usage load between sites, to improve efficiency by sharing programs and data, and to make it easier to develop and support software jointly.

The early networking period, from the mid-1950s to the mid-1960s, saw the introduction and wide adoption of modems and other communications hardware, as well as the development of various experimental, one-of-a-kind systems to connect terminals with computer centers. Remote interactive computing thus became a reality for thousands of users. There were relatively few networks that connected computers with each other, however, and incompatibility between different types of computers severely limited this form of networking. The aim of these early networks was to allow users to share computing power or common databases. Communication between users was not yet an important focus of networks.

The ARPANET and Internet

There was a major change in both the technology and the application of computer networks with the ARPANET and Internet. The Internet is a worldwide system of interconnected computer networks that links thousands of machines and millions of computer users. The Internet has its roots in an experimental computer network called the ARPANET that was built by the U.S. Defense Department's Advanced Research Projects Agency (ARPA). Because of the strategic military role of computers, ARPA became one of the major funding sources for computer science in the early 1960s. By the late 1960s, ARPA was funding research centers around the country to work on projects such as timesharing, artificial intelligence, and graphics.

In 1966, Robert Taylor, who was in charge of computing research at ARPA, began discussing the idea of a nationwide computer network to link the agency's various research sites. The goals of the project were to save computing costs by allowing researchers at different sites to share computers, programs, and data; to advance the state of the art in computer science; and to encourage communication and collaboration between researchers in different locations. Work on the ARPANET began in 1969 under the leadership of Lawrence Roberts, and the network was up and running by 1972. A number of corporate and university contractors designed, built, and tested the hardware and software for the network (see figure 10.1).

The communications infrastructure of the ARPANET was a set of minicomputers connected by leased telephone lines. The minicomputers (called Interface Message Processors, or IMPs) provided an interface for computers and terminals to connect to the network. They also guided data through the network using a novel technique called packet switching. The first minicomputer had been introduced by Digital Equipment Corporation in 1963, and by 1969, minis were cheap enough that it was feasible to consider devoting several of them to running a network.

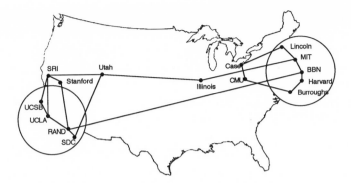

Figure 10.1. The ARPANET in April 1971. Based on data from Bolt, Beranek, and Newman reports.

In a packet-switching network, the data to be transmitted is divided into small units called packets. Each packet has a header containing its source and destination addresses as well as some control information. The ARPANET IMPs used this information to route the packets to their destination and to reassemble them into the proper order. The advantage of sending individual packets, rather than having a continuous connection between the source and destination computers, is that the communications links can be used more efficiently. Packets from different connections can be interleaved on the same link, so that transmission capacity is not wasted when a connection is idle. Also, packets from the same connection can be sent to their destination by different routes, making it possible to distribute traffic among multiple links or respond to a breakdown in one part of the network by routing traffic elsewhere. Thus packet switching makes efficient use of expensive telephone connections while also potentially increasing the reliability of the network.

Packet switching was a fairly new idea in 1969. It had been proposed in the early 1960s by Paul Baran of the Rand Corporation, but no network had been built on his design. In the United Kingdom, Donald Davies of the National Physical Laboratory had independently invented the idea in 1966, and the NPL begun work on its own packet-switching network shortly before ARPA. But there was quite a bit of skepticism that packet switching would be successful, because of the complexity involved in routing and reassembling packets. Thus one of the most important contributions of the ARPANET to the history of networking was that it provided one of the first practical demonstrations of packet switching. The project also made several other contributions to the state of the art. It showed that different types of computers could be connected in the same network, which had required overcoming compatibility problems; it solved many of the problems of distributed networking, such as routing; and it developed many important protocols for establishing and managing network connections.

All of this laid the groundwork for the successor to the ARPANET: the Internet. Following the success of the ARPANET, ARPA embarked on other experiments that adapted packet switching for use with other media. The agency built a mobile radio network, which had obvious advantages for military field use, and a satellite network, which could cover a large area at a high transmission rate. However, while ARPA's three networks all used packet switching, they were very different in design: ARPANET had point-to-point links, while the other two were broadcast media; the radio network had mobile terminals; and the satellite links had higher data rates and a wider area of coverage than terrestrial nodes. This left ARPA with a dilemma: how to make it possible to exchange data between three such diverse networks.

To solve that dilemma, ARPA initiated a program to develop techniques for connecting networks, a process known as internetworking. Program managers Vint Cerf and Robert Kahn decided that special computers called gateways would be placed between networks; the gateways would do any necessary translation between the different network formats, and would also decide how to route data across networks. Cerf and Kahn realized that in order for different types of networks to communicate, they would need to share a common set of procedures; this set of procedures was called the Internet Protocol (IP). They also developed a companion protocol called the Transport Control Protocol (TCP), which regulates the interaction between host computers; this set of common protocols became known as TCP/IP. The set of networks connected by gateways and communicating using TCP/IP forms a single metanetwork—a network of networks—called the Internet.

The theory behind TCP/IP was that the Internet should make very limited demands on each network: as long as a network could meet minimal performance standards, its internal design could vary widely. Thus TCP/IP could provide the common bond between the diverse defense networks. But this also meant that TCP/IP was potentially very attractive to other computer users who might need to connect dissimilar machines or networks. This gave users an alternative to manufacturers' networking products, which were also being introduced in the mid-1970s. In 1974, IBM launched its Systems Network Architecture; Digital began offering DECNET in 1976, and various other vendors followed. But these systems were designed to work only with machines from that vendor, and they were not open to user modification. Because the

Internet protocols were nonproprietary, performed well, and could accommodate a range of network types, they were widely adopted by other research and commercial networks, often in conjunction with proprietary network systems.

The mid-1980s saw the Internet expand beyond the ARPA research community. One of the first steps was the creation in 1982 of CSNET, a network for computer science researchers that was funded by the National Science Foundation and used the ARPANET as part of its infrastructure. While the ARPANET was restricted to ARPA's own contractors, CSNET membership was open to any computer science institution—academic, commercial, nonprofit, or government—willing to pay dues. Then in 1985, NSF decided to build a network to connect its supercomputing sites. NSF and ARPA came to an arrangement whereby ARPA would make the Internet available to NSF researchers until the new NSFNET was ready; then the NSFNET, which had a higher data capacity, would take over the ARPANET's role as the backbone of the Internet. This changeover occurred between 1988 and 1990, at which point the original ARPANET was retired. The creation of NSFNET helped extend ARPANET access to most of the major universities in the country, and a number of links were also made to overseas research sites.

The final step in broadening access to the Internet came in the early 1990s, when the U.S. government arranged to shift the administration of the Internet to the private sector. This allowed the network to be used by commercial enterprises as well as government-sponsored researchers, and made commercial public network services possible. The current Internet has a decentralized structure: local networks are connected to regional, national, and international networks provided by a number of commercial or government operators. Thus no one organization owns or operates the Internet. The technical management of the Internet is done by the Internet Engineering Task Force, a loosely organized body that is open to all interested parties and works out technical standards on a consensus basis.

Several factors in the technology and environment of the Internet seem to have contributed to its success. Liberal funding from the government got the project started at a time when the technologies were not attractive to corporations. Because the essential technologies and protocols were developed with public funding, they became freely available, which encouraged their wide adoption. On the technical side, the system is decentralized, which allows it to scale up without a lot of coordination and without creating bottlenecks, and the system was designed to be flexible. The ARPANET accommodated a wide variety of computers; the

Internet accommodates a wide variety of networks and demands only the lowest level of performance from each one. Without the ability to grow and change in unpredictable ways, the Internet would certainly not be the omnipresent technology it is today.

Local Area Networks

Local area networks (LANs) are relatively small networks that are usually owned by a single organization, such as a business or university. Since cost and complexity tend to be problems for small networks, special techniques have been developed to make LANs relatively simple and inexpensive by eliminating the need for switches.

One of the precursors of LAN technology was the University of Hawaii's ALOHANET. The university had a single computer center and several scattered campuses, and needed a way to connect them despite a lack of good phone connections between campuses. The ALOHANET approach was to broadcast the packets on a radio frequency. The ALOHANET used two radio channels: one channel was used to carry traffic from the central computer to the various user terminals, and the other channel carried all the traffic from the user terminals to the computer center. The question was, with all the terminals broadcasting on a single channel, how could they avoid interfering with one another?

The solution had a brilliant simplicity: don't try to prevent collisions at all—just make sure the system can recover from them. The ALOHA system was called a random access method because access to the channel by different terminals was not scheduled or coordinated; each terminal transmitted on its own initiative. If two users happened to transmit packets at the same time, both packets would be garbled. If that happened, each terminal would retransmit the packet. To avoid retransmitting at the same moment and endlessly repeating the collision, the terminals would wait for a random period of time before retransmitting; in all probability, the two terminals would choose different times to retransmit and thus avoid another collision. This provided a simple way to share the radio channel without having to coordinate the actions of all the terminals.

A Ph.D. student in computer science at Harvard named Robert Metcalfe learned about the ALOHANET and decided he could improve on it. In his 1973 dissertation he described his insight that varying the retransmission interval in response to traffic loads could radically improve the throughput of the system. When he graduated, Metcalfe got a job at

Xerox PARC, where a group was building an experimental graphical workstation called the Alto. Given the job of creating a network to connect the various Altos at Xerox PARC, Metcalfe designed a faster, more efficient version of the ALOHANET, using a shared cable instead of a radio channel, which he called Ethernet. This became the first local area network.

Ethernet rapidly became the standard for LANs in offices and universities. Ethernet does not require any packet switches, because there is no routing; every packet is broadcast to every computer. The only equipment needed is a simple piece of cable and an interface board for each computer, making the system relatively inexpensive and easy to install. These advantages account for the popularity of Ethernet for small-scale networks.

A different type of LAN that is often used in manufacturing is the token-passing LAN. The two main types are the token ring, developed by IBM, and the token bus, developed by General Motors and other manufacturers for factory automation. In these types of LANs, a "token" (a short message) is passed around from one computer to another. Holding the token gives a computer permission to send data; since only one computer has the token at any time, there are never any simultaneous transmissions, and hence no collisions. Token networks are popular in automation applications because they are predictable: unlike Ethernet, where there is no guarantee (just a high probability) that a message will eventually get through without a collision, token systems guarantee that each computer will be able to send its message within a definite period of time.

The World Wide Web

The mid-1980s saw a new development in the United States: the rise of commercial online services such as CompuServe, America Online, and Prodigy that were aimed at ordinary people, rather than businesses or researchers. These were not originally conceived as networking services, but rather were large timesharing services. They appealed to recreational computer users because of their custom-built, user-friendly interfaces, which were more akin to the easy-to-use personal computer interfaces than ordinary timesharing systems. The services they provided included free software, access to online shopping or other services, and the opportunity to "chat" in real time with other customers of the service. Shortly after these commercial online services had established themselves, the privatization of the Internet made it possible for them to offer Internet access as part of their service. This introduced the Internet to a vast new audience of ordinary people who were exploring the possibilities of using networked computers for education, recreation, and personal interaction.

Soon after the general public discovered the Internet, they began to hear about an exciting new development called the World Wide Web, which rapidly became one of the most popular services supported by the Internet. The web is a collection of interactive, multimedia information that can be accessed over the Internet. A typical web page is a screenful of text and graphics related to a particular subject, with links to other pages. The ability to create links between different documents is called hypertext; the web combines hypertext with multimedia (text, images, audio, and video) to create a "hypermedia" system. The program that retrieves and displays web pages is called a browser, while the computers that store the information are web servers.

The roots of the web are quite different from those of the ARPANET and Internet. The idea of hypertext was proposed by Ted Nelson, a counterculture figure of the 1960s and 1970s who championed the idea of bringing computers to the people in a manifesto entitled *Computer Lib*. Well before it was technically feasible, he predicted widespread ownership of personal computers with graphical interfaces and envisioned a worldwide database of linked information. Nelson worked on developing various hypertext systems and inspired many people with his notion of user-friendly computing.

One of the people who drew on Nelson's idea was Tim Berners-Lee at CERN, the European laboratory for particle physics, which had taken an early interest in developing network technologies due to the peculiar needs of its users. High-energy physicists need to travel to accelerator sites such as CERN to do their experiments. While they are there, they generate huge amounts of data, and they need to communicate with, and transfer data to, their home institution. Thus CERN had installed its own local area networks and was connected to various wide area networks as well.

Berners-Lee appreciated the value of these networks, but he felt that the exclusive use of text in most network applications was a severe limitation. He wanted to create a system that would help scientists collaborate by making it easy to create and share multimedia data. In 1990, Berners-Lee created the first version of this new type of system, which he dubbed the World Wide Web. The web consists of all the browsers, servers, and web pages that are connected using the Internet. The main features that make information sharing on the web possible are a common language for creating web pages, called hypertext markup language (HTML); a common protocol for exchanging information, called the hypertext transfer protocol (HTTP); and a standard address format, called the uniform resource locator (URL).

The web proved extremely popular with the scientists at CERN, and it soon spread to other research sites in the international physics community, including the U.S. National Center for Supercomputing Applications (NCSA). In 1993, an NCSA team led by Marc Andreessen began developing an improved web browser called Mosaic. Unlike the original web software, Mosaic could run on smaller machines— workstations and personal computers—and was distributed free of charge. This made the web accessible to the general public for the first time, and usage began to grow at a phenomenal rate. Within a few months there were a million or more copies of Mosaic in use, and web traffic increased almost 10,000 times between November 1992 and March 1994. Andreessen and his team left NCSA to work on a commercial version of Mosaic called Netscape; other commercial browsers followed and continued to fuel the rapid growth of the web. The appealing graphical format, the opportunity to create their own web pages, and the ability to discover interesting information using links and search tools all made the web popular with ordinary people around the world for both work and entertainment.

Conclusion

The history of networks reflects a number of trends in the history of computing. Like many other computer technologies, networks received an early boost from government and military funding. Local area networks show how the idea of networking was adapted to practical considerations like cost, reliability, and simplicity. And the web, like the personal computer, became popular by satisfying the demand for a user-friendly graphical interface, and encouraged the use of computers for recreational as well as serious purposes. Network technologies helped transform the computer from a calculating machine for the few to a communications medium for the many.

FOR FURTHER READING

Janet Abbate, *Inventing the Internet* (Cambridge, Mass.: MIT Press, 1999). [A scholarly history of the Internet.]

Tim Berners-Lee, *Weaving the Web* (San Francisco: Harper, 1999). [A history of the World Wide Web by its inventor.]

Robert M. Metcalfe, *Packet Communication*, edited by Peter H. Salus, *Computer Classics Revisited* (San Jose, Calif.: Peer-to-Peer Communications, 1996). [A retrospective on Metcalfe's original work that led to the Ethernet.]

Arthur L. Norberg, and Judy E. O'Neill. *A History of the Information Processing Techniques Office of the Defense Advanced Research Projects Agency* (Minneapolis: The Charles Babbage Institute, 1992). [A scholarly history of the early Internet as well as other computing areas funded by the U.S. Defense Department.]

Andrew S. Tanenbaum, *Computer Networks*, second edition. (Englewood Cliffs, N.J.: Prentice Hall, 1989). [A textbook that combines historical background with technical explanations.]

11

Computer Interfaces

Susan B. Barnes

A human–computer interface is the point of interaction between a person and a digital computer. In early computers, the interface included punched card technology, keyboards, and text-oriented commands. With the introduction of graphical interfaces, the technology expanded to include the mouse, windows, icons, and visual commands.

Interacting with Early Computers

Before computers were machines, they were people. Human computers performed scientific calculations using mechanical calculators, books of tables, drafting tools, and pencil and paper. Human computers working on scientific calculations were a small number of people compared to those working in business-related activities such as accounting and inventory control. In the first half of the 20th century, the work of this latter group was often performed with the aid of punched card machines. Early computing machines used punched cards as a method of interaction. The use of punched card technology came to the attention of the American public back in the 1890s when Herman Hollerith developed a punched card system that was used for the U.S. Census (see figure 11.1).

During the first half of the 20th century, American businesses had increasingly installed punched card equipment. These machines performed tasks that had previously been accomplished by people with

Figure 11.1. On the cover of the August 30, 1890 issue of *Scientific American*, illustrations of people (referred to as "enumerators") were shown working on the punched card system developed by Hollerith. Courtesy of Smithsonian Institution, National Museum of American History.

the help of adding machines, desktop calculators, key-operated accounting machines, and addressing machines (see figures 11.2 and 11.3). Ten-key punched card tabulators were little more than giant adding and sorting machines. These machines could handle accounting chores that

Figure 11.2. Hollerith redesigned his tabulator to incorporate an adding mechanism. Cards were redesigned with columns of numbers that allowed the use of a single 10-key punch for all applications. Courtesy of IBM Archives.

Figure 11.3. Bell Laboratories developed a series of relay calculators composed of standard telephone relays that used teletype terminals to input and output data. An operator is using the Complex Number Calculator (circa 1940). Property of AT&T Archives. Reprinted with Permission of AT&T.

went beyond the abilities of hundreds of human clerks. In steel mills, department stores, factories, and government offices, mechanical calculators became a basic piece of office equipment.

During World War II, IBM helped the government develop mechanical computing devices by sponsoring the Mark I project with Harvard University. But the computer that captured the attention of the nation was ENIAC, developed at the University of Pennsylvania. This was the first large-scale electronic computer, which had data fed into it by punched cards. In addition to punching cards, human operators had to manually set switches to program the machine (see figure 11.4). For over a decade after ENIAC, punched cards were the main input devices, and for over two decades, teletype machines were the most common output devices. For example, the first digital computer shown on American television, UNIVAC, used punched card technology. It was used in a broadcast to predict the 1952 presidential election (see figure 11.5). In the broadcast, UNIVAC was described as a "computer." Since that time, the meaning of the word "computer" has come to denote machines, not people.

Both ENIAC and UNIVAC were designed by John W. Mauchly and J. Presper Eckert, Jr. The former was built to help perform complex calculations for the war effort. In contrast, the latter was built as a commercial product. At the end of World War II, the mainstay of mechanized business data processing was still the punched card accounting machine. But after World War II, computers started to be developed for a variety of business applications. These large machines were kept in back offices.

The Postwar Era and Interactive Computing

Computer interfaces have progressed through several styles of interaction. The first method used the batch processing of punched cards as a form of interaction. With batch processing, people supplied instructions to computers on punched cards and then waited hours or days until their cards were able to be processed. A second method called interactive computing supported the relative access to computers. The technologies needed for interactive computing were developed in government-funded projects during the 1950s and 1960s.

The biggest government project of the 1950s postwar period was the SAGE (Semi-Automatic Ground Environment) air defense system. This developed out of the Whirlwind project started at MIT in 1943 (see figures 11.6 and 11.7). Whirlwind parallels the development of the computer. When the project started, its purpose was to create analog flight-training simulators. During the development process, SAGE

Figure 11.4. Two women changing the plug board wiring and function table values of the ENIAC before punched card data is input into the computer. Courtesy of Sperry Corporation Archives.

Figure 11.5. In 1952, the UNIVAC computer was used to predict the presidential election. In this picture, J. Presper Eckert, Jr. is showing Walter Cronkite how the machine works. Courtesy of Hagley Museum and Library.

Figure 11.6. The 1951 Whirlwind control room. Operators viewed real-time information displayed on cathode ray tubes. A light pen enabled operators to select display features. Courtesy of MIT Corporation Archives.

Figure 11.7. SAGE, the 1960s air defense system, converted radar information into computer generated pictures. Operators could select information by pointing with a light pen at the appropriate target displayed on the screen. Courtesy of the Charles Babbage Institute, University of Minnesota, Minneapolis.

became computerized. In later years this project introduced magnetic core memory to store information, timesharing, and software to run the computer's cathode-ray tube (CRT) terminals. Radar information was converted by SAGE into computer-generated pictures, and the light pen was introduced as a method of computer interaction. The light pen enabled an operator to select information by simply pointing to the appropriate target displayed on the CRT screen.

The type of computer interaction developed by Whirlwind and SAGE was further advanced in the early 1960s at MIT. In 1960, J. C. R. Licklider, an MIT psychology professor, wrote a paper called "Man-Computer Symbiosis." In his paper he proposed that a new relationship between people and computers was needed. He argued that people should be able to "think in interaction with a computer." Following this vision, Ivan Sutherland, a graduate student at MIT, did a thesis called "Sketchpad." Sutherland was working on the problem of getting information from the computer to be displayed on various kinds of display screens. He was developing a direct relationship between bits of information stored in a computer's magnetic memory and pixels (picture elements) or dots of light displayed on a screen.

In 1962, Licklider became the head of ARPA's Information Processing Techniques Office that provided government funding for computer projects. One of the projects that he funded had been proposed by Douglas C. Engelbart, a computer scientist working at the Stanford Research Institute (SRI). In 1968, Engelbart demonstrated his concept of interactive computing to a group of computer scientists (see figures 11.8 through 11.10). The technologies Engelbart presented include windowed screen design (displaying information in boxes on the screen), the user interface (interacting with text and graphics in real time), hypertextual linking of documents (making associative connections between documents), the mouse (a hand-held device to manipulate data), collaborative computing (sharing documents stored in a computer system), and multimedia (using a computer screen to display text, graphics, and video). It has taken the computer industry over 20 years to integrate many of the features Engelbart first demonstrated in the 1960s.

Business Machines and Personal Computing

By 1970, IBM dominated the computer industry. To compete with IBM, Xerox decided to set-up a research facility to invent the "office of the future." They established Xerox PARC (Palo Alto Research Center) and hired computer researchers away from government-funded projects.

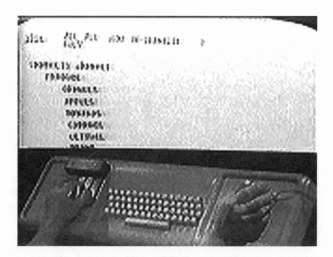

Figure 11.8. Douglas C. Engelbart's 1968 keyboard with a standard typewriter keyboard in the middle, a five-button chord keyset on the left, and a mouse on the right. (Photo obtained from low-resolution video capture.) Courtesy of Douglas Engelbart.

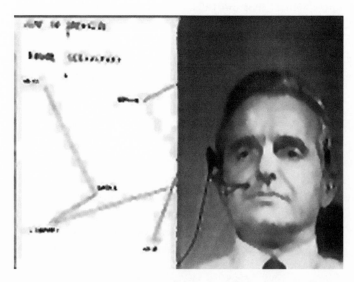

Figure 11.9. During the 1968 demonstration, Engelbart explained how his interactive system could link information. Engelbart co-invented hypertext links with Jeff Rulifson. In the 1990s, hypertext became the foundation for the development of the World Wide Web. (Photo obtained from low-resolution video capture.) Courtesy of Douglas Engelbart.

Figure 11.10. The Smalltalk-80 programming system invented at Xerox PARC. It is a graphical interactive approach to object-oriented programming (circa 1982). (Photo obtained from low-resolution video capture.) Photo courtesy of Xerox Corporation, Palo Alto Research Center.

At PARC, research in interactive computing was applied to business systems. The PARC researchers moved computers from the back room to the front office. They invented the concept of "personal computing." To make computers easier for office workers to operate, Alan Kay and his team invented graphical interfaces. Their work was inspired by Engelbart and also by Logo, a programming language invented to help children use computers. Xerox's Alto and Star office systems had graphical interfaces. Graphical interfaces use icons and a mouse to interact with computers instead of typing in verbal commands. Xerox researchers succeeded in inventing many of the features of today's personal computers, but their systems were not commercially successful (see figure 11.11).

While Xerox was inventing the office of the future, hardware hackers in California were trying to bring computers to the people. The personal computer revolution started outside of the development of mainstream computing. Introduced in 1977, Apple Computer's Apple II was an instant commercial success.

Early personal computers retained the structure and look of mainframe computers by using command-line interfaces (figure 11.12). In 1979, after a visit to Xerox PARC, Steve Jobs saw the possibility of using graphical interfaces to make computers "user-friendly."

Figure 11.11. In 1981, Xerox introduced the Star Office Automation System with its radical user interface that introduced icons, the desktop metaphor, windows, and direct manipulation to officer workers. It came with a standard keyboard surrounded by function keys on the top, left, and right. Photo courtesy of Xerox Corporation, Palo Alto Research Center.

Figure 11.12. The Apple II became the first successful personal computer for business and home use. It had a command-line interface with standard keyboard. Courtesy of the Charles Babbage Institute, University of Minnesota, Minneapolis.

He immediately went back to Apple and applied the technology to the Lisa office system under development at Apple. By the time the Lisa was introduced, IBM had already released the IBM Personal Computer which quickly became the computer of preference for office workers. On their

Apple Computer's new Macintosh: extraordinary computing power and exceptional ease of use. Macintosh's main unit, which weighs less than 17 pounds, contains a 32-bit microprocessor, a built-in 3½-inch disk drive, a 9-inch black-on-white display, 64K of ROM and 128K of RAM. Equipped with a detachable keyboard and a mouse pointing device, Macintosh fits quickly and easily into the work style of businesspeople, professionals and students. The suggested retail price for Macintosh is only $2,495.

Figure 11.13. The original Macintosh introduced in 1984 brought "user-friendly" graphical interface technology to personal computer users. Courtesy of the Charles Babbage Institute, University of Minnesota, Minneapolis.

second try, the Macintosh, Apple introduced the first commercially successful graphical user interface (GUI, pronounced goo-ey) for personal computers (figure 11.13).

In the 1980s, a variety of different companies attempted to introduce graphical and window-styled interface technology for the IBM-PC standard. The most successful was Microsoft's Windows. One other notable computer system was the Amiga 1000 introduced in 1985 by Commodore (figure 11.14). Originally designed as a video game machine, the Amiga combined video and computer technology together in "desktop

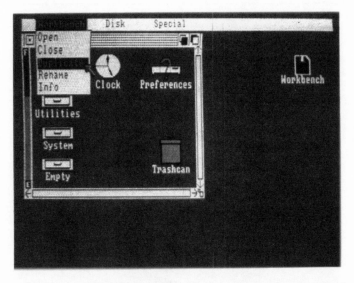

Figure 11.14. The Amiga 1000 enabled users to interact in both graphical and text-based windows. This multitasking system was the first personal computer to integrate video and support multimedia.

video." Its design was unique because it supported color graphics, sound, multitasking, and both graphical and command-line interfaces.

Going Gooey (GUI) and Beyond

In the late 1980s the computer industry began a migration from command-line to graphical interfaces. From personal computers to workstations, the industry was going "gooey." A variety of new interface designs were under development including NeXTSTEP (NeXT, Steve Jobs's Company after he left Apple), Open Look (Sun, AT&T), OSF/Motif (Open Software Foundation), OS/2 (IBM), and Windows (Microsoft). But it was the success of Windows 3.0, introduced in 1990, that made graphical interfaces the most common form of human–computer interaction (see figures 11.15 through 11.17).

Graphical interface technology continues to advance as more multimedia and Internet features are added to personal computers. Command-line style Internet access has been replaced by two new innovations: the World Wide Web and graphical browsers. In 1990, the web first introduced hypertextual linking as a way to access documents across the Internet. Three years later, Mosaic (an earlier version of Netscape) revolutionized Internet access by allowing people to access information

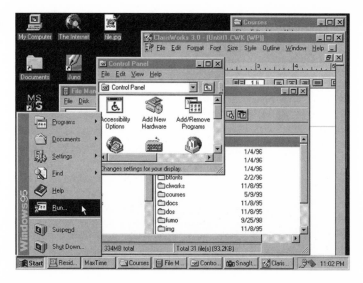

Figure 11.15. During the 1980s, Microsoft introduced several versions of their Windows software, but not until the introduction of Windows 3.0 was the program successful. Windows 3.0 made graphical interface technology available to IBM standard personal computer users. Depicted here is the Windows 95 interface that followed. Screen shots reprinted by permission from Microsoft Corporation.

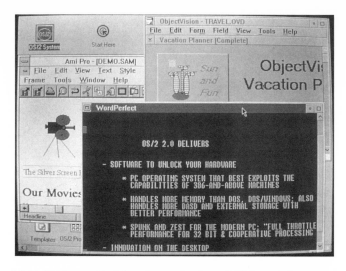

Figure 11.16. IBM's graphical interface technology OS/2 has tried to compete with Windows in the marketplace to become the graphical interface standard for personal computers. This picture illustrates its multitasking capabilities. Courtesy of IBM Archives.

Figure 11.17. After leaving Apple Computer, Steve Jobs started developing the NeXT computer system. NeXTSTEP combines a graphical user interface with object-oriented development tools. (Object-oriented software programming is a method of writing programs that relate to an object, rather than writing one-at-a-time line programs. Independently programmed objects work together like building blocks.) In 1989 the original World Wide Web software was developed by Tim Berners-Lee using a NeXT computer. Courtesy of The Computer Museum History Center.

Figure 11.18. Netscape revolutionized the Internet by enabling people to access information through a graphical interface. Courtesy of Netscape Communications Corporation.

through a graphical interface (see figure 11.18). Now graphical interfaces are adding audio, video, and voice recognition features to human–computer interaction.

ACKNOWLEDGMENTS

This chapter was based on "The Development of Graphical User Interfaces from 1970 to 1993," a New York University doctoral dissertation by Susan B. Barnes, 1995.

FOR FURTHER READING

Susan B. Barnes, "Douglas C. Engelbart: Developing the Underlying Concepts for Contemporary Computing," *IEEE Annals of the History of Computing,* 19/3 (1997): 16–26.

Lee Butcher, *Accidental Millionaire: The Rise and Fall of Steve Jobs at Apple Computer* (New York: Paragon House, 1989).

Martin Campbell-Kelly and William Aspray, *Computer: A History of the Information Machine* (New York: Basic Books, 1996).

Paul Carroll, *Big Blues: The Unmaking of IBM* (New York: Crown Publishers, 1993).

Charles Eames and Ray Eames, *A Computer Perspective: Background to the Computer Age* (Cambridge, Mass.: Harvard University Press, 1973, revised/paperback ed. 1990).

Charles H. Ferguson and Charles R. Morris, *Computer Wars: How the West Can Win in a Post-IBM World* (New York: Random House, 1993).

Adele Goldberg, *A History of the Personal Workstation* (New York: ACM Press, 1988).

Alan Kay, *Doing with Images Makes Symbols: Communicating with Computers* (Stanford, Calif.: University Video Communications, 1987). [Videotape].

Brenda Laurel, *The Art of Human–Computer Interface Design* (Reading, Mass.: Addison-Wesley Publishing Company, 1990).

Steven Levy, *Insanely Great: The Life and Times of Macintosh, the Computer That Changed Everything* (New York: Viking, 1994).

Stephen Manes and Paul Andrews, *Gates: How Microsoft's Mogul Reinvented an Industry—and Made Himself the Richest Man in America* (New York: Doubleday, 1993).

Frank Rose, *West of Eden: The End of Innocence at Apple Computer* (New York: Penguin Books, 1989).

John Sculley with John A. Byrne, *Odyssey: Pepsi to Apple . . . The Journey of a Marketing Impresario* (New York: Harper & Row Publishers, 1988).

Douglas K. Smith and Robert C. Alexander, *Fumbling the Future: How Xerox Invented, Then Ignored the First Personal Computer* (New York: William Morrow and Company, Inc., 1988).

Randall E. Stross, *Steve Jobs & the NeXT Big Thing* (New York: Atheneum, 1993).

12

Computers in Use

Frederik Nebeker

I n the 1950s and 1960s, computers became much more numerous, and the individual computer became increasingly prominent—both massive itself and attached to bulky "peripherals" (a term dating from the mid-1960s to denote the auxiliary devices, usually for input or output, attached to computers). The trend to increasing numbers of computers accelerated in the 1970s and 1980s, but most computers were much less prominent, as suggested by the names "minicomputer" and "microcomputer" (which date from the late 1960s and the early 1970s respectively). In the 1990s, the computer, in the form of the microprocessor, became both ubiquitous and, in most applications, invisible.

This historical curve of visibility was paralleled by a curve of obtrusiveness. Most of the early calculating aids, such as slide rules and desk calculators, fit readily into their work settings. With the unwieldy electronic computers of the 1950s and 1960s, however, the workplace was altered to accommodate the computer or was even organized around it. Miniaturization of electronics in the last three decades of the 20th century made the computer once again, in most cases, fit into a workplace whose physical arrangement was determined by other considerations.

Here we will look at four different settings for computers: offices, the military and aviation, factories, and homes and schools. These will provide examples both of how computers were shaped by their uses and of how certain activities have been shaped by computers.

Computers in Offices

Offices, almost by definition, are places of information processing. As described in chapter 2, an office-machine industry has provided a wide variety of information-processing devices for more than a century. Here we see visual evidence of one constant element: desks bearing one breadbox-sized device each. Clerks, accountants, and most anyone else dealing with a great deal of numerical information were grateful for adding machines (figure 12.1). Later came the more versatile calculating machines, capable of multiplication, and typewriters, which became the most common office machine.

Punched card tabulating equipment, originally developed by Herman Hollerith for processing the 1890 U.S. census, did not fit easily on a desktop. One sat at a machine (or moved from one machine to another) rather than setting a machine on one's desk (figure 12.2). For three-quarters of a century, until the 1970s, offices continued to use punched cards for data processing. The machinery underwent continual improvement throughout this time. There were new capabilities, such as printing and multiplying, and new types of machines, such as duplicating punches and verifiers (see figure 12.3). And in 1933, IBM introduced removable control panels, so that it became easier to change the sequence of operations of a tabulating machine.

The SABRE airline reservation system pioneered many techniques of a large-scale, dispersed, real-time computer system. It drew upon the experience with an earlier system, SAGE (see pp. 136–139). Airline

Figure 12.1. Felt & Tarrant adding machine in use in about 1910. Source: Felt and Tarrant handbook, 1914.

Figure 12.2. A Census Bureau worker operating a Hollerith Pantograph machine. The data that were placed onto punch cards with the Pantograph could be read by the early Hollerith tabulating machines. Courtesy of U.S. Census Bureau.

Figure 12.3. The payroll department of the Realsilk Company in 1941, showing several types of Remington-Rand equipment in use: card punches at the left, a printing tabulator in the center, and a sorter at the right. Courtesy of Hagley Museum and Library.

reservations were first arranged using telephones and paper records. Then came a computer system that used teletype terminals (figure 12.4). In 1968, this system was handling 100,000 calls a day. Later the information was displayed and processed using video display units.

Computers have come to play large roles in newspaper and book publishing, in movie production, and in television broadcasting. In direct-to-plate publishing, text is written, edited, and laid out with illustrations, all electronically, and the computerized page images are used to create the printing plates. Computers have changed movie production, especially through computer graphics, and television broadcasting (see figure 12.5).

Computers for Aerospace and the Military

Aviation, space exploration, and national defense all involve many information-intense activities. One of the first military tasks that required automatic calculation was the direction of long-range guns. In the Spanish–American War (1898) and the Russo-Japanese War (1904–1905) naval battles typically took place at a range of 4000 yards, but during World War I many encounters were at ranges of nine miles or more. Accurate direction of the guns required taking into account the direction

Figure 12.4. The computer-based SABRE airline reservation system used teletype terminals before video terminals came into use. Source: American Airlines.

Figure 12.5. The WJXT newsroom. There are as many computers or computer terminals as people. Photo by A. J. Shurelds. Courtesy of WJXT.

Figure 12.6. The M-9 undergoing field trials. Note the trackers operating a separate unit in the background. Property of AT&T Archives. Reprinted with Permission of AT&T.

and range of the target ship, its motion, and the motion of the firing ship as well. By the time of the war, sophisticated electromechanical computers had been developed to carry out this task.

In World War II the rapid motion of airplanes posed even greater challenges for fire control. During the war, engineers at Bell Telephone Laboratories and elsewhere built an automatic fire-control system called the M-9 that used radar tracking of the target (figure 12.6). The M-9 was an analog computer with electromechanical and electronic components. It was especially effective against the German V-1 "buzz bombs" directed against London.

Another task that demanded automation was code-breaking. During World War II a variety of code-breaking computers were developed in different countries. The Germans used an automatic encoding device called the Enigma. The Allies built a machine, called the Bombe, that could simulate the Enigma, rapidly trying different settings (see figure 12.7). The most impressive code-breaking computer was the Colossus, built at Bletchley Park in England. A special-purpose electronic digital computer, Colossus contained 2500 electron tubes; hence it

Figure 12.7. A woman of the U.S. Naval Security Group Command in Washington, D.C. operating an N-530 Bombe in May 1945. Courtesy of National Cryptologic Museum/National Security Agency.

is regarded as the first large electronic computer. It became fully operational in the spring of 1944, and by the end of the war, 10 of these machines were in use at Bletchley Park.

The first large-scale general-purpose electronic digital computer was the ENIAC, designed during World War II to calculate ballistic tables (the numerical tables used by artillerymen in aiming their guns) and built at the University of Pennsylvania (figure 12.8). Completed in 1946, the ENIAC contained some 18,000 electron tubes and was programmed by setting switches (of which there were 6,000) and plug-cords. In the late 1940s, the ENIAC performed calculations for a wide variety of purposes, including hydrogen-bomb design and weather forecasting.

Familiar to many people through the Star Tour ride at Disneyland and Disney World, flight simulators required high-speed calculation. figure 12.9 shows an experimental flight simulator from about 1950.

One of the largest and most influential computer systems in the first decades of electronic computing was the air defense system known as SAGE (Semi-Automatic Ground Environment). It involved monitoring data in real time from widely separated radar stations. The system was developed in the early 1950s at MIT's Lincoln Laboratory and tested in what was called the Cape Cod System (whose direction center is shown in figure 12.10). The radar sets and monitors were connected by telephone

Figure 12.8. ENIAC project member Arthur W. Burks and a programmer in 1946 checking a program on the ENIAC. Courtesy of Arthur W. Burks.

Figure 12.9. This flight simulator was built for the Viscount aircraft in about 1950. Source: Science Museum/Science & Society Picture Library.

Figure 12.10. SAGE control center. Courtesy of MITRE Corporation Archives.

Figure 12.11. Astronaut Sally Ride aboard *Challenger* in June 1983. Courtesy of NASA.

lines to the Whirlwind computer. The SAGE system was one of the first uses of the electronic digital computer in a real-time control system.

The space program used computers in numerous ways, such as design, communications, guidance, and onboard control. When the integrated circuit made hand-held calculators feasible, astronauts on NASA's Space Shuttle used them for many tasks, such as to calculate orbital position, to process experimental data, and to act as an alarm clock (see figure 12.11). Most of the time during a flight, each astronaut carried a calculator in his or her pocket.

Computers in Factories

In Aristotle's *Politics* we read, "if every instrument could accomplish its own work, obeying or anticipating the will of others ... if the shuttle would weave and the pick touch the lyre without a hand to guide them, chief workmen would not need servants, nor masters slaves." More than 20 centuries later, the computer has helped realize Aristotle's vision.

Automation has gone farthest in the processing industries. Sensors of various types made it possible to monitor, in a central location, what was going on throughout a factory, and actuators, such as valves and heaters, could also be controlled centrally. So when computers became available, it was possible in many cases to automate ordinary operations (see figure 12.12).

Figure 12.12. A control room of the Rail Products and Pipe Division of Bethlehem Steel in Steelton, Pa. Courtesy of Bethlehem Steel Corporation.

Even in the fabricating industries, computers have come to play important roles, most spectacularly in robots, machines that mimic the behavior of humans. Japanese automobile manufacturers have been leaders in the use of robots (see figure 12.13). Computer control has also made possible fully automated warehouses (figure 12.14).

Computers in Homes and Schools

Though university campuses were the sites of many of the earliest computers, relatively few students made much use of them. Then came

Figure 12.13. The GMFanuc S-380 robot in operation. The S-380 was designed for spot welding, but has also been used for material handling. Courtesy of Fanuc Robotics.

Figure 12.14. A fully automated warehouse at the CIBA plant in Switzerland in 1969. Courtesy of Novartis AG.

Figure 12.15. Timesharing, using teletype terminals, at Dartmouth College in the mid-1960s. Courtesy of Dartmouth College Library, Special Collections.

Figure 12.16. In the mid-1980s personal computers began to appear in large numbers in elementary schools. In this photo, children are using the Xerox Alto. Courtesy of Xerox Corporation, Palo Alto Research Center.

timesharing: simultaneous use of a computer by a number of users at remote locations. Beginning in the mid-1960s, college students were often able to run programs and, later, to do word processing from terminals at various locations on campus. The first terminals were

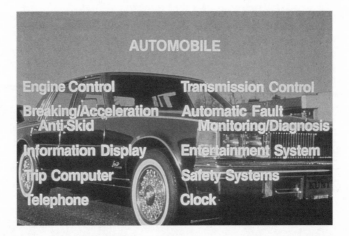

Figure 12.17. In the mid-1980s, microprocessors were used in many ways in automobiles. Courtesy of Intel Corporation.

teletype machines, essentially electric typewriters that printed both what the student typed in and what the computer outputted (see figure 12.15). Later cathode-ray-tube terminals made it easier to interact with the computer.

Beginning around 1980, the personal computer came to college campuses and to primary and secondary schools (see figure 12.16). The personal computer was, of course, made possible by the microprocessor, which has also allowed signal-processing and information-processing capability to be embedded in instruments, vehicles, and appliances (see figure 12.17). The computer has, in most of its applications, become invisible.

FOR FURTHER READING

Charles Eames and Ray Eames, *A Computer Perspective: Background to the Computer Age* (Cambridge, Mass.: Harvard University Press, 1990).

Tom Forester, ed., *The Information Technology Revolution* (Cambridge, Mass.: MIT Press, 1985).

Steven Lubar, *Infoculture: The Smithsonian Book of Information Age Inventions* (Boston: Houghton Mifflin, 1993).

III

The Computer Industry

13

The Modern Computer Business

Arthur L. Norberg

The electronic digital computer industry emerged tentatively onto the world stage in 1946, with the founding of two engineering companies, Eckert-Mauchly Computer Corporation (EMCC) and Engineering Research Associates, Inc. (ERA), and the incorporation by several large firms of the new electronic computing ideas into their planning. Only a handful of large firms participated in this new computer phenomenon: IBM, Raytheon, Bendix, and Burroughs. The small startup engineering firms included EMCC (1946), ERA (1946), and later California Research Corporation (1950). And this was just in the United States. In the United Kingdom, the established business machines company British Tabulating Machine Company (1902) and the new companies Lyons & Company (1947), Ferranti Company (1948), Elliott Brothers (1949), and English Electric (1949) all entered the emerging industry. As Continental Europe and Japan recovered from the devastation of World War II, new computer companies sprang up in the 1950s in these regions as well. For example, in France, Compagnie des Machines Bull gradually entered the electronic and digital computer business starting in 1948. Similarly, Japanese engineers built computers in the 1950s, and a number of companies—Fujitsu and Nippon Electric among them—joined with university laboratory personnel to design new computers. In the United States, it was especially the small firms with an engineering emphasis in leadership and capability that provided stimulus to the early computer industry. These businesses were organized at a time before a stable computer design was available, and they participated in the development of standard schemes for designing, manufacturing, and servicing computers.

Electronic Computing in the Immediate Postwar Years

Virtually all the designs of the period, in the United States and abroad, were based on the ideas incorporated into the EDVAC design, developed at the University of Pennsylvania. This chapter focuses on the pattern of development fostered by a few companies in the United States. Except for work in Switzerland based on Konrad Zuse's computers and some development in the United Kingdom following design of the Colossus during World War II, most international work could be traced back to the ENIAC and EDVAC developed at Pennsylvania. The Office of Naval Research was partly responsible for the spread of computing information about ENIAC and EDVAC through sponsorship of a series of lectures at the Moore School of the University of Pennsylvania in the summer of 1946 and a symposium at Harvard University in January 1947. The focus in these meetings was on hardware design. Applications emerged from the interests of commerce, government, and military users. The details of how European and Japanese developments mirrored those in the United States can be obtained by consulting items on these regions in the Further Reading list.

The search for a production-model computer design by personnel in these firms is the key to understanding this early history. In the quest for a stable design, emphases were placed mostly on speed, storage, and reliability. Early computer designs were slow, had small storage, and were insufficiently reliable to encourage faith in this practicality. Speed could be increased in two ways: decreasing interaction time of parts of the computer, such as reducing distances electrical signals must travel, and increasing the amount of data and instructions stored inside the machine. Thus, an array of development programs in companies and universities pursued techniques to increase storage and decrease the time to isolate a single data element, keeping costs in mind in most cases. This search culminated in the development of magnetic core memory by MIT, IBM, and Harvard, which swept the international industry in the mid-1950s (see figure 13.1). The need for reliability in components led to new developments also. Industry developed a range of new components suitable for use in computers, including mass production techniques for their manufacture. Designers crafted more stable circuits for the transfer of data and instructions internally.

Figure 13.1. A magnetic core memory storage panel. Typical of the panels used in the late 1950s, this example was the type used in Sperry-Rand computers of the period. Courtesy of the Charles Babbage Institute, University of Minnesota, Minneapolis.

We shall examine three of the significant companies in the early digital electronic computer business in the United States: Eckert-Mauchly Computer Corporation, Engineering Research Associates, and IBM. None of them defined clear and achievable objectives for engineering development in 1946; they came to them only over time. Overarching objectives—the major components of a design—were apparent to the participants in computing, but operational objectives for making and integrating these components were not. An adequate state of knowledge about computing was just developing. Indeed, it took a decade to arrive at sufficient knowledge to develop the operational objectives that helped each company to construct a design that could be produced in large numbers. Along the way, all the firms interested in digital computing machines struggled with pushing back the envelope around the known into the unknown. And the accumulated experience of the personnel in these firms influenced the definition of problems investigated and the solutions proposed.

In the received history of the early computer industry, writers have assumed that EMCC in Philadelphia possessed the capability and an advanced state of knowledge, which should have given them an edge. This edge, they say, was reduced by the inability to convince potential funders and purchasers. Some authors have also assumed that IBM resisted devices that would affect the tabulator market, and when they realized it might take away their market share, they entered the market late with dedication and overwhelmed the smaller firms. Engineering Research Associates is seen as occupying its own niche defined with the United States Navy, and it only entered the commercial area in the early 1950s after a Navy computer they designed seemed appropriate for the commercial market. In fact, all three of these companies struggled with computer ideas in the early years, because they needed to learn a great deal about how to implement designs for data processing and to produce a digital computer system, and their search was similar to that of companies in other countries.

Computers and Commerce in the United States

In June 1946, the National Bureau of Standards (NBS) submitted a proposed contract to EMCC that involved a phased approach to acquisition of a computer. The three phases were research and design, building and testing of components, and construction of a machine. The contract, a copy of which is in the Sperry Collection at the Hagley Library, accepted by EMCC in September, called for the company to

> supply the necessary qualified personnel and facilities for and prepare plans, specifications, and wiring diagrams for an automatically sequenced electronic digital computing machine or machines suitable for general mathematical computations and for preparation of census reports, and construct and test such models of components as may, in the opinion of the Contractors or Scientific Officer, be necessary to insure the adequacy of these plans and specifications.

Eventually, this was understood by the contracting parties to mean the construction and demonstration of two components: a delay-line memory device and a magnetic tape input/output device.

The nature of these components was dictated by EMCC's knowledge of the problems to be solved on such a machine, an investigation that had been going on since April 1944 by John Mauchly. In 1946 and 1947, EMCC staff visited Northrup Aviation and the Prudential Insurance Company. Over time the attention to similarities and differences in problems to be solved honed the designs for the elements required by the contract.

At the end of the six months following receipt of the NBS contract, it was clear to EMCC that more time would be needed for R&D. A two-day conference was held at EMCC to evaluate progress. Mostly, EMCC was concerned about input/output and sorting speed. They considered reducing the size of the storage devices to decrease retrieval time there (this would double the number of vacuum tubes to be used); running input and output tapes simultaneously (which involved more control circuitry); going further than this and maintaining simultaneous running of internal operations and tape reading and writing; and trying to develop ways to transfer input/output data in blocks rather than word by word. After considering the changes in equipment required for each of these options, they concluded that reduced storage device size and simultaneous running of internal operations and input/output devices were feasible.

The EMCC engineers constructed scale models of basic circuits, as well as an electronic clock for control of the tapes. The devices for controlling intermittent tape feed were also in the test stage. Needless to say, they were far from ready to submit "plans, specifications and wiring diagrams for an automatically sequenced electronic digital computing machine." And money was becoming critical.

In mid-May 1947, EMCC presented a proposal to the Prudential Insurance Company to build a machine for them. The proposal contained a detailed description of the hardware and the programs to be used in operation of the machine. Detailed design specifications were presented for the tape system and how data would be recorded on the tape, the typewriter operation and speed, the memory size of delay-line memory, and the methods of checking. They also offered some comments on the manner of operation of the control circuits. In June, EMCC received a contract from the Prudential. And in July, they received an order from the Northrup Company to build a different but somewhat similar computer. The machine construction used to develop the ideas for all three machines was called the BINAC. The accomplishments of the BINAC development were similar in character and process to that of projects pursued simultaneously by ERA and IBM.

The U.S. Navy funded the organization of Engineering Research Associates in St. Paul, Minnesota, for the purpose of inventing data processing equipment for naval intelligence uses (see figure 13.2). In contrast to EMCC, ERA concentrated on designing equipment to serve specific data needs of the Navy as defined by the Navy, and later to serve the needs of the newly organized National Security Agency as well. The 3M company, also in St. Paul, worked on similar magnetic materials for recording tape devices and supplied some research materials to ERA for magnetic tape and drums. Engineering Research Associates employed a number of physicists and electrical engineers with experience in magnetic devices. To handle large amounts of data, they focused on magnetic tapes and drums with read–write capabilities. The company received its first

Figure 13.2. The main ERA R&D and manufacturing facility in St. Paul, Minnesota, in the 1950s. Courtesy of the Charles Babbage Institute, University of Minnesota, Minneapolis.

contract from the Navy in February 1946. By June 1946, ERA had organized several projects related to the search for a better data storage system. One of these projects was to analyze the use of photographic film as a potential tape source. Another was to examine solid-state delay lines as a storage medium. Yet another focused on the use of magnetic media as a storage source, the primary area of personnel talent. Eventually, ERA emphasized only magnetic media, even though under the Navy's urging they continued to investigate other possible storage media.

In its first proposal to the U.S. Navy in the winter of 1946, ERA wanted to focus on three areas of investigation. First, ERA wanted to make an assessment of the type and nature of problems arising in the Navy amenable to solution on data processing machines. This type of investigation would generate information about the similarities and differences among problems with an eye toward reformulating them to fit the machines "recently developed" and understanding the required accuracy and amount of storage. The problems not solvable by known machines could be used for a second area of investigation: decisions about "the direction of development of the computing machine art." The third area would involve ERA in the design and construction of the various components needed for new solutions. The proposal went on to discuss what ERA saw as the first problem needing attention: storage. "The storage problem is one of the most difficult in building computing machines," it said.

In a few months, from sometime in mid-1945 to March 1946, ERA people—Howard Engstrom, Charles Tompkins, Lawrence Steinhardt, and John Howard in particular—had analyzed this new field and reached the level of the EMCC and Institute for Advanced Study groups in an appreciation of the nature of the problems involved in design and construction of computing machines. This proposal shows that the ERA group was just as thorough as the other two groups in identifying the nature of the problems and carving out a promising direction.

The machine to incorporate these ideas was codenamed Goldberg. Goldberg was analogous to EMCC's BINAC in the role it played in ERA's path to the ERA 1101 system. The sorting out and education processes that occurred from mid-1946 to mid-1947, when Goldberg was ostensibly finished, allowed ERA to learn the field of computing, accumulate the engineering skills to pursue research and development on an organized and sustained basis, and carve out for itself an area of computing machine development that would have an important influence on the field. Thus, the critical years in ERA's growth were 1947 and 1948. In these years they changed from an electronic project shop to a computer design company.

Following a strategy similar to EMCC and IBM (and, we might add, Northrup and Technitrol Engineering), ERA built prototypes of components. In May 1947, John Coombs prepared a memorandum for Howard Engstrom containing a proposal to build a model storage system for demonstration. "It seems to be ERA policy," he wrote, "to obtain publicity for the magnetic storage drum." But he felt "reticent" about this, "because we have not developed, nor will we develop on this project, the associated electronic circuits essential for a storage device of the type in which most of our potential customers or competitors are interested."

The success of the Goldberg prototype resulted in a modification of the ERA contract to develop a slightly different system for drum storage called Demon, five of which were delivered to the National Security Agency in October 1948 followed by one Goldberg. In the meantime, ERA's effectiveness brought them the contract of their dreams: to design and develop a complete computer. Over the next two years, ERA designed and built a computer for the National Security Agency—Atlas, which with some modifications became the commercial ERA 1101.

The admirable histories of IBM tell us that IBM followed a strategy for digital electronic computer development in the same years of 1945 to 1948 as EMCC and ERA. When a number of IBM researchers returned from the war, they brought with them ample knowledge of the new electronic technology. Immediately they set about to introduce it into IBM products present and future. Mid-way through World War II, Thomas Watson, Sr., recognized the need to pursue electronic solutions in the development of future products, and he took advantage of the return from military service of Ralph Palmer, Steve Dunwell, and Thomas Watson, Jr., to introduce the latest electronic ideas to the company. Watson, Jr., and several IBM people visited the ENIAC laboratory early in 1946. They came away convinced that electronic digital techniques were the wave of the future.

In the period 1946 to 1948, IBM personnel built the Selective Sequence Electronic Calculator (SSEC) and set about modifying other equipment to fit into new configurations, such as the Card-Programmed Electronic Calculator (CPC), that would take advantage of electronic speeds and reliability. By 1948, a series of projects had been initiated at IBM that would result in their first computers of the 1950s. I refer to the cathode-ray tube (CRT) memory project, the data processing test assembly, and the Tape Processing Machine (TPM). All of these projects were built around the recognition that to take full advantage of electronic circuitry required a great deal more storage than was available in earlier calculating machines. In this account, the Tape Processing Machine project is the most interesting. In the TPM project, IBM not only developed a storage drum similar to that of other firms, but it deliberately measured itself against ERA, the perceived leader in storage drum technology (see figure 13.3).

By mid-1949, IBM considered the developing EMCC UNIVAC machine to be a substantial threat, because of EMCC's promotion of it as a business machine. Palmer, Dunwell, and Nathaniel Rochester believed that IBM should "design and build a large-scale, tape-oriented machine" for business purposes. By doing so, they could assess reliability of such a design and evaluate the benefit of tape compared with cards. In May 1949, IBM had decided to adapt a magnetic drum storage unit to its 604 electronic calculator, but by August there were no tangible results from this effort. John McPherson, director of engineering, concluded that it would be as difficult to adapt the drum to the 604 as it was to design the 604 originally. He and others discussed the possibility of buying from ERA a drum and the services to adapt it. In September, IBM decided to follow a double path: inaugurate a tape processing machine project to include drum development and contract with ERA for drum work.

The preliminary design for the TPM done by Rochester was finished by March 1950. The design called for a CRT memory of 2000 characters, an optional drum for faster-than-tape storage, an unspecified number of magnetic-tape units, and a stored-program system with a repertoire of

Figure 13.3. An ERA public relations photograph taken in the early 1950s to illustrate the size range of magnetic storage drums for sale and used in ERA/Remington-Rand computer systems. These drums are very similar to those used by other manufacturers such as IBM. The men in the photograph are the people largely responsible for the concept and design of the drums and their operating circuitry. From left to right: John L. Hill, Arnold A. Cohen, Frank C. Mullaney, Robert Perkins, Arnold Hendrickson, and William R. Keye. Many of these men became principals in the new Control Data Corporation in 1957. Courtesy of the Charles Babbage Institute, University of Minnesota, Minneapolis.

about 40 single-address instructions. Additional CRT storage of 200 characters (the capacity of a single tube) was termed accumulator storage. As built over the following two years, the machine builders did not achieve what was an ambitious plan for the time.

What made IBM and ERA different from EMCC was the resources they could draw on. Within the company, IBM could support R&D on computers because of their successful tabulator business; ERA had the support of the U.S. Navy; EMCC had neither of these resources. The areas of government and business EMCC relied on for support were cautious about when success would be achieved and held back somewhat. In addition, EMCC had a range of problems unconnected with machine design.

In order to work out operational objectives for computer design in the crucial years of the early industry—1946 to 1949—IBM, ERA, and EMCC placed emphasis on similar storage system problems. In the case of IBM this was the Tape Processing Machine; for EMCC it was the BINAC; and for ERA the project was called Goldberg. Each firm followed the same technical strategy, which can be summarized as follows:

1. Personnel used their knowledge of earlier ENIAC and EDVAC developments as their springboard for future design. But this left open many design questions, both in hardware and software.
2. Personnel surveyed the technical field to evaluate the suitability and the need for modification of parts of computer system design.
3. They modified components to achieve simplicity and reliability in their new design.
4. They evaluated the tradeoffs in design by study of the interfaces between system modules.
5. Following good engineering practice, they constructed component modules for testing and redesign. It was these parts they demonstrated to the agencies with which they had contracts.
6. Finally, they constructed a full machine, and although I did not describe the process of repeated modification of serial machines, no two machines over the next several years were alike.

From this brief history, we learn first that the starting point for the three companies was the same: they all emphasized storage systems development first. For ERA, the storage system was an end in itself, but it developed into a project for a complete machine—the Atlas and the 1101. For both EMCC and IBM, storage systems were also starting points in a longer program to produce a computer. None of the companies, indeed no project anywhere, had a sufficient knowledge of how to build functioning computer storage elements or any part of the machine to ensure success. The transfer of information among the projects played a particularly important part in ERA's activities. Information transfer was also significant to IBM, but less so to EMCC, though they did benefit from attendance at the various conferences held in the late 1940s.

Second, the strong interaction between designers and users in the determination of machine specifications and functioning ability has up to now not been examined by historians so as to give equal weight to both sets of people. Users' demands have been treated in the literature as reactionary, whereas designers' ideas have been portrayed as revolutionary. In fact, the roles of NBS, the Census Bureau, and the Prudential Insurance Company in EMCC's design and planning were critical to bringing a functional machine to market; EMCC's contracts were designed by them to converge with and at the same time meet customer demand. The view in 1946 that such a device could be constructed from standard radio parts did not prepare the designers or the anxious users for the large number of obstacles the designers needed to overcome before an operating machine became available. Many design changes occurred along the way, and a number of components and test instruments needed to be newly designed and built for proper performance in computer systems.

The U.S. Navy played a different role for ERA. Navy contracts provided a systematic learning and R&D period for ERA, during which they could advance from smaller to larger scale system contracts. While IBM's start may be considered slow from some perspectives, the time frame for bringing the machine to market is about the same as for EMCC and ERA. Its objectives were quite different than those of EMCC, even though they were somewhat similar in their ends—to obtain commercial customers for the new machinery. The approach of IBM to the development problem was quite different from EMCC's, and in some respects different from ERA's. In at least one instance, IBM's R&D program converged with ERA's, and IBM even contracted with ERA to pursue design of magnetic drums for use in IBM machinery. This contract held out the possibility of significant commercial business for ERA, and might have spelled the difference between independence and absorption, except that IBM decided to go it alone and finance their own development. This decision was reached after much discussion within the company about customer needs and market potential.

Eckert-Mauchly Computer Corporation began with a general design for a computer based on the work of its two founders at the University of Pennsylvania. Eckert and Mauchly helped to define the early general outline of a machine, and their team's subsequent work culminated in the justly famous UNIVAC of the 1950s. Engineering Research Associates organized to design and develop data processing machinery to advance the state of the art beyond wartime devices. International Business Machines, the only company of the three to have a commercially installed base of calculating equipment and therefore a base to protect, in the late 1940s cautiously pursued a strategy of R&D that would enhance and add to their markets. By 1951, each had a computer to market; all three machines were important designs; and each contributed substantially to an understanding of speed, storage, and reliability of computers.

Establishment of the Computer Business

The early 1950s saw the sale or rental of very few computers for commercial use. In the last half of the 1950s, the rate of computer use grew considerably. While a part of this increased use resulted from improved computer design and hardware, there can be little doubt that much of this growth resulted from the availability of trained computer professionals—many from the military and government establishments, and others who were trained within the growing numbers of commercial and industrial computer centers.

The development of commercially oriented computers was a long and painful process. Early military-based computers were designed for narrow purposes and generally intended to solve just one class of problem (such as artillery firing, message decoding, and nuclear device detonation). They were generally designed specifically for the immediate needs of each individual user. Little, if any, thought was given to making one computer's operating system compatible with another's. Nor, in the early days, did computer manufacturers consider it necessary to supply operating software for the machines they made: that was the responsibility of the purchaser.

Computer manufacturers—if the construction of machines on a one-at-a-time basis can be said to constitute manufacturing—were hardly in a financial position to develop and design totally new computer systems. Thus, the early computers offered on the commercial market were basically adaptations of computers developed for the military. They were very expensive, large machines, with small memories, and generally limited to one rather narrow range of applicability.

Potential commercial and business users found computers a baffling challenge. In spite of the tremendous promise of computers for handling payroll, inventory, and other essential functions with far greater speed and accuracy than before, business firms rarely had one person, much less a sophisticated staff, who had any idea of how to program or operate a computer.

Though many industrial executives began to appreciate the potential value of computers in business in the early 1950s, it was exceedingly hard for them to see how to actually begin using the new technology. To meet this problem, IBM developed the practice of supplying a staff of computer programmers and operators, along with other components of the computer's installation, to those customers who leased large IBM machines. These IBM staffs performed the computer programming and operated the machine while training an in-house staff of computer professionals for the customer. They also created a strong dependence on IBM by the customer, virtually ensuring future computer leases by the customer from IBM. But EMCC, later Sperry-Rand, used a different technique. A team of programmers and analysts visited a potential customer, and after surveying the customer's data-handling procedures, designed an entire programming system for use by the company.

This, too, helped to tie the customer to one company as the program worked only on Sperry-Rand computers. The responsibility for software was slowly shifting to the manufacturer.

It wasn't until the mid-1950s that IBM and others realized that their business would benefit if the computers they manufactured were supplied with appropriate software and manuals. Computer information and programs began to be shared among user groups promoted by both IBM and the UNIVAC Division of Sperry-Rand. As the technology advanced in the early 1960s, computers less and less operated on a "batch process" basis in which a single set of data and its processing program had to be read into the computer at the same time: computer memory capacity became large enough to retain operating programs, which could be called up as needed. Compatibility among machines and timesharing became features of machines in the 1960s. This greatly increased the efficiency with which a computer could be operated.

Finally, early in the 1960s, there began to appear a "critical mass" of trained computer personnel and "computer savvy" industrial managers, so that industries began to have confidence in incorporating computers into the fabric of their operations. At the same time, IBM, UNIVAC, Honeywell, Philco, and other firms, began to offer a new class of commercially oriented computer having much greater breadth of utility— many with engineering/science utility as well as business utility. By the mid-1960s, it was possible to say that a commercial computer market was in evidence—after 20 years of broad government stimulation and financial support. Subsequent advances in both hardware and software have been manifold, culminating in the introduction of the personal computer in the 1980s, spearheaded by Apple.

NOTES

The various proposals, contracts, and other documents quoted or cited in this article may be found in the Sperry Corporation Records at the Hagley Library and Museum in Greenfield, Del. In 1955, the Sperry Corporation merged with Remington-Rand, which had already acquired EMCC and ERA, to form the Sperry-Rand Corporation. Sperry-Rand, in addition to sustaining the operations of ERA and the Univac Division, integrated electronic computer technology into the firm's extensive military products and systems. Specific items pertaining to this chapter may be found in the Sperry Corporation Records (Accession 1910), Part I, Harry Vickers presidential papers (1942–1967) and Part II, minutes and administrative papers; and Sperry Corporation, Univac Division, Engineering Dept. Records (Accession 1825).

FOR FURTHER READING

Charles J. Bashe, Lyle R. Johnson, John H. Palmer, and Emerson W. Pugh, *IBM's Early Computers* (Cambridge, Mass.: MIT Press, 1986).

Martin Campbell-Kelly, *ICL: A Business and Technical History* (Oxford: Clarendon Press, 1989).

Martin Campbell-Kelly and William Aspray, *Computer: A History of the Information Machine* (New York: Basic Books, 1996).

Franklin M. Fisher, James W. McKie, and Richard B. Mancke, *IBM and the U.S. Data Processing Industry: An Economic History* (New York: Praeger, 1983).

Kenneth Flamm, *Creating the Computer: Government, Industry, and High Technology* (Washington, D.C.: Brookings Institution, 1988).

Bruno Leclerc, "From Gamma 2 to Gamma E. T.: The Birth of Electronic Computing at Bull," *Annals of the History of Computing*, 12/1(1990): 5–22.

David E. Lundstrom, *A Few Good Men From Univac* (Cambridge, Mass.: MIT Press, 1987).

Arthur L. Norberg, Judy E. O'Neill, and Kerry J. Freedman, *Transforming Computer Technology: Information Processing for the Pentagon, 1962–1986* (Baltimore: Johns Hopkins University Press, 1986).

Kent C. Redmond and Thomas M. Smith, *Project Whirlwind: The History of a Pioneer Computer* (Bedford, Mass.: Digital Press, 1980).

Nancy Stern, *From ENIAC to UNIVAC: An Appraisal of the Eckert–Mauchly Computers* (Bedford, Mass.: Digital Press, 1981).

Sigeru Takahashi, "Early Transistor Computers in Japan," *Annals of the History of Computing*, 8/2(1986): 144–154.

14

Computers in the Marketplace

Martin Campbell-Kelly

To date, the business history of computer firms has not been very sophisticated. While there are a few good institutional histories of IBM, there are no first rate monographic studies of the other old-line computer firms such as NCR, Remington-Rand, or Burroughs.[1] For new computer firms such as Microsoft, Intel, and Apple, the situation is far worse. As Doron Swade of the London Science Museum has noted:

> General historiography of modern computing has been commandeered by the oracles of the immediate—journalists—who regale us with tales of Californian misfits who catapulted themselves from garages into multi-nationals in less than a decade. The sensational rise of Apple and Microsoft, of Wozniak, Jobs and Gates has become a parable of entrepreneurial success.[2]

The aim of this essay is to address some aspects of economic and business history as they relate to the computer industry. It considers three topics. The first topic is the rise of the old-line computer firms and the concept of organizational capabilities. As the popular press constantly reminds us, IBM and Microsoft are very different animals: the one is old, stuffy, and bureaucratic, while the latter is young, lively, and reactive. All true, but our analysis needs to be deeper. If IBM is really so bureaucratically fossilized and inept, then how did it manage to hold its dominant position for nearly a century? The second topic is entrepreneurship. The recent genre of computer biographies focuses strongly on personalities such as Bill Gates and Steve Jobs, but the level of analysis is often superficial, and most of this writing is not far removed from the long discredited "great man" school of history. Thirdly, and lastly, the essay will look at new computer firms and the Silicon Valley phenomenon. If one wants to understand and write about the firms that begat the PC revolution, then the best place to start is with the recent literature on networked firms and external capabilities.

Organizational Capabilities and the Rise and Fall of IBM

International Business Machines (IBM) was founded (initially as the Tabulating Machine Company) in 1896. For almost a century it seemed the company could do no wrong. Between the two world wars it dominated the punch card machine market, and from the 1960s it dominated the computer market—first in mainframes, and later in PCs, software, and services. Then, from about 1990, everything seemed to go wrong. In January 1993, IBM reported the largest corporate loss in history.

There have been several books analyzing IBM's fall from grace. Typical of the genre, and perhaps the best known, is Paul Carroll's *Big Blues*.[3] In essence, Carroll's thesis is that IBM had got fat and happy and was so sluggish with bureaucratic inertia that it could not move fast enough to compete in the new world of desktop computing. Carroll's explanation is true to a degree, but it is superficial. The fact is that IBM was no fatter, happier, or more complacent than it had been in most periods of its past. What had changed was the environment in which IBM operated, and the organizational capabilities it had developed over nearly a century were no longer sufficient to ensure such easy dominance of the information-processing market.

We need to dig deeper to understand how IBM got to be so big and successful in the first place. The eminent business historian, Alfred D. Chandler, has noted that from the middle of the 19th century:

> The visible hand of management replaced the invisible hand of market forces where and when new technology and expanded markets permitted a historically unprecedented high volume and speed of material through the processes of production and distribution.[4]

Chandler's thesis is that big firms were the engines of economic growth in the United States in the second half of the 19th century and for most of the 20th century; IBM is paradigmatic of this thesis. Chandler argues that firms such as IBM became increasingly self-sufficient through "vertical integration," which eliminated the costs and uncertainties of dealing with other suppliers. For example, buying components from an external supplier entailed the transaction costs of purchasing, verification of price and quality, as well as a margin of profit for the supplier. To eliminate these costs, IBM integrated backward, progressively undertaking virtually all its own manufacturing. By the 1930s, IBM was, in effect, taking bars of steel and reels of copper wire in at one end of the production process and shipping out punch card machines at the other. It also forward integrated into sales and marketing, rather than using selling agents. In this respect, IBM was following practices pioneered by firms such as Singer Sewing Machine and National Cash Register.[5]

Chandler's thesis has been further refined by the concept of *organizational capabilities*, which can be defined as the "human and organizational knowledge that enables business institutions to produce goods and services." Easily the best discussion of IBM's organizational capabilities has been given by business historian Steven Usselman, who identifies the following capabilities within IBM, which existed prior to its entry into the computer market:

- Sales and marketing expertise
- Market research and knowledge
- Flexible electromechanical production
- Systems integration know-how
- Business systems and applications knowledge
- Maintenance and field engineering competencies.[6]

The company had established all these capabilities in the 1930s. The change caused by the emergence of the mainframe computer was not nearly so radical as is often supposed: "The only significant difference between large electromechanical data-processing installations and these machines was that computers would use vacuum tubes instead of electromechanical relays and would involve a staggering amount of wiring. But these differences appear trivial when placed in the total context of the task." [7] Not only that, but by the late 1940s, IBM already had a modest development and manufacturing capability in electronics, having produced a series of electronic calculating-punches. The approach of IBM to computers was evolutionary rather than revolutionary: the company already had all the capabilities it needed to succeed in the electronic data-processing computer market, apart from a modest boost to its electronics development and manufacturing facilities.

It is important to contrast IBM with firms such as RCA and General Electric, which both made entrees into computing in the 1950s. These firms had capabilities in electronics, but hardly any of the other business and marketing capabilities identified above. It was simply not possible for them to develop relevant competencies at the speed that the market demanded, and so by the early 1970s they finally had to concede defeat and withdraw from computer manufacture. It is tempting to suppose that it was just a matter of buying or developing new competencies, but as many writers have observed, capabilities grow and mature slowly and cannot be instantly created on demand.

How does the concept of organizational capabilities help us to understand IBM's demise in the early 1990s? It can be argued that, manufacturing apart, all of IBM's capabilities amounted to a problem-solving competence. The company was famous for selling solutions to business problems rather than equipment. In an uncertain world where electronic data-processing expertise was thin on the ground, customers were only too willing to pay a hefty premium to have their hand held and their problems solved by IBM. In the 1980s, however, the environment began to change. Increasingly, IBM's specialist knowledge was captured by software, and the emergence of open standards made the integration of computer equipment an increasingly easy task. For example, if an insurance company wanted to install an information system, there were many software packages to choose from, and many systems integrators who could put together a suitable hardware/software solution. So IBM could no longer offer any unique expertise to command its premium prices. And IBM was even less needed in the new world of desktop computing, since it required no proprietary expertise to install a network of computers. The fact is that by 1990, hardly anyone needed IBM anymore.

It is interesting that since about 1995, IBM has bounced back, its stock price having quadrupled from its low point. While some of this improvement can be attributed to rationalization and downsizing, the new network-centric computing environment has been the most important factor. With the emergence of the World Wide Web, intranets, and Computer Supported Cooperative Work (CSCW), the corporate computer center is faced with new uncertainties, and IBM's hand-holding is once again appreciated by a market lacking in confidence. The lesson here is that IBM will prosper just so long as its existing organizational capabilities fit the market environment.

Entrepreneurship

Since the early 1980s, when the personal computer entered the public consciousness, there has been a vast popular literature on the history of computing. Much of this literature consists of biographies—or hagio-graphies—of key figures in the commercial development of the information technology (IT) industry. Individuals receiving the biographical treatment include J. Presper Eckert and John Mauchly, Kenneth Olsen, Seymour Cray, An Wang, Larry Ellison, Adam Osborne, Scott McNeally, Steve Jobs, and (inevitably) Bill Gates.

Almost all of this literature has been produced by journalists and is generally heroic in tone. In most of these books, the entrepreneurial career follows much the same trajectory: a young (usually male) technophile sees an opportunity to make some IT artifact; he starts production in a small way; he secures venture capital and the firm grows rapidly; and there is an initial public offering which makes our hero personally rich. More often than not, the career trajectory then takes a nose dive: sooner or later the entrepreneur stumbles, and he is ousted by the board of directors.

Compelling as much of this literature is, it leaves unanswered some key questions. For example, why is the United States (and especially the West Coast) such a rich source of entrepreneurs, in comparison with Japan and Europe? How much of an individual's success can be attributed to luck, and how much to heroic personality traits? How does entrepreneurship in the IT business compare with other sectors—such as biotech, or even non-high-tech sectors? Why do so many entrepreneurs ultimately come unstuck and lose control of the firms they created?

Of course, individual authors have individual explanations for their heroes, but what historians want is a more general understanding. The economic literature can provide us with some explanations. One of the more accessible academic treatments of entrepreneurship is Mark Casson's *Entrepreneurship and Business Culture*.[8] However, perhaps a better starting point for those unfamiliar with the economic literature is John Kao's *Entrepreneurship*, which includes a number of case studies from the IT sector.[9] Kao offers the following definition:

> Entrepreneurship is the attempt to create value through the recognition of business opportunity, the management of risk-taking appropriate to the opportunity, and through communicative and management skills to mobilize human, financial, and material resources necessary to bring a project to fruition.[10]

There are three key issues here: the recognition of a business opportunity; the appropriation of resources; and entrepreneurial creativity. I will consider these in turn.

Recognition of the business opportunity is the starting point of the entrepreneurial trajectory. The entrepreneur sees what others do not see, or sees it before others see it. This *information asymmetry*, as economists term it, is usually achieved through proximity to the source of an invention, which gives the entrepreneur an early start, before the knowledge has diffused to potential competitors. Almost every IT entrepreneur can be seen to have such special knowledge at the outset of their entrepreneurial career. For example, Eckert and Mauchly were able to recognize the business opportunity represented by the computer because they had been involved in it for at least two years before the technology became widely known. Ken Olsen saw the opportunity for low-cost computers through his intimate connections with MIT. Again, all the early personal computer entrepreneurs had intimate knowledge of the potential of the microprocessor months or years before it became diffused beyond Silicon Valley. And most recently, we have observed the case of Marc Andreessen, who formed the Netscape Corporation on the basis of knowledge gained while working at the National Center for Supercomputing Applications (NCSA) in the University of Illinois. In all these cases, recognition of the business opportunity owed a great deal to sheer luck—being in the right place at the right time. (This should be a comfort to the majority of us who are not entrepreneurs.)

In business startups based on a technical innovation, human resources are a sine qua non—about which I will have more to say in the next section. Of course, the availability of human resources is only one issue; they still have to be paid for, and entrepreneurs rarely have independent financial means.

In the United States, the development of venture capital institutions since the 1950s has been crucial to the entrepreneurial startup. For example, the lack of venture capital was largely responsible for the demise of the Eckert-Mauchly Computer Corporation in 1949, when Eckert and Mauchly's sponsor, the president of American Totalisator, died in an aircraft accident. Unable to find another benefactor, Eckert and Mauchly eventually had to sell their business to Remington-Rand, where it became the Univac Division. Ironically, in the same year, General Doriot of MIT was in the process of establishing American Research and Development (ARD), the first venture capital (VC) firm in the United States.[11] When Ken Olsen came to establish the Digital Equipment Corporation in 1957, he was much more fortunate than Eckert and Mauchly, because he received an initial injection of capital from ARD. How that original investment of $70,000 grew to become $400 million is one of the defining episodes of computer history.

There is, however, more to venture finance than money: the leading venture capital firms also helped nurture and provide wise counsel to young entrepreneurs. For example, Ken Olsen was initially advised against entering the computer business when DEC was formed in 1957, but instead to concentrate on producing circuit boards. Only when the firm had developed into a significant corporation did it go into computer manufacturing in 1962. The counseling role of the venture capitalist is well documented in the histories of the personal computer startups of the 1970s and 1980s. For example, at Apple Computer the mature wisdom of Mike Markkula was a vital counterweight to Steve Jobs's youthful exuberance. This added value of the U.S. venture capital industry is a critical factor that was not seen in many similar operations in Europe and other countries; often they had money to lend but were unable to provide the wisdom to use it well.

After the initial venture funding, much greater financial resources will eventually be needed by the successful enterprise. Thus the next key financial event is the initial public offering (IPO). At this point the startup is poised in size between a modest partnership and a major corporation. For the IPO, a whole network of financial intermediaries and institutions come into play. The typical outcome of the IPO is that the entrepreneur and his team receive their first major financial rewards, and shares in the company are publicly traded on one of the smaller equity markets. The IPO enables the entrepreneur to liquidate what have up to this point been only paper assets. The IPO is a key cultural phenomenon that legitimates the whole entrepreneurial process, and it provides an encouraging potential exit mechanism for other would-be entrepreneurs. In time, as the company grows and matures, it can expect to gain access to the primary equity markets in the United States and eventually overseas. But by that stage, the entrepreneur will typically have moved on to some other enterprise or will have changed his role to that of a manager.

The distinction between entrepreneurs and managers is one of the key concepts of the entrepreneurship literature. The key personality traits and tasks of the entrepreneur include:

- Charismatic leadership
- Visionary and intuitive mindset
- Risk-taking and managing
- The ability to capture and orchestrate human and financial resources
- An obsessive attention to detail ("the devil is in the details").

These are very much the heroic qualities that the biographies of IT entrepreneurs dwell upon. These are the essential traits needed to establish a company up to the size of perhaps a hundred employees. It is during the next phase of growth that problems typically set in—when the firm grows to a thousand or more employees and has a turnover exceeding a $1 billion. The typical personality traits and tasks of the manager include:

- Trusteeship of other people's assets
- Status seeking, within a hierarchical organization
- Seeking after personal wealth and security

- Rational rather than intuitive personality
- Task delegation.

The contrasting personality traits of the entrepreneur and manager make it very easy to classify people such as the following pairs: IBM's Herman Hollerith and Thomas Watson Sr.; Univac's J. Presper Eckert and James Rand Jr.; or Apple's Steve Jobs and Gil Amelio.

There are, however, a tiny number of individuals who have succeeded in being both entrepreneur and manager. Either they have combined the roles of entrepreneur and manager, or have seamlessly evolved from one into the other. Good examples are David Packard, Ken Olsen, and Bill Gates. It must be recognized that these are truly exceptional individuals, quite different from "mere" entrepreneurs or managers.

Networked Firms and External Capabilities

In the United States, the large-scale, vertically integrated corporation is a post-Civil War phenomenon. In the antebellum period, technologically sophisticated products were generally created though the cooperation of networks of small specialized firms. This form of industrial organization was more prevalent in England, whose industrial revolution predated that of the United States by half a century.

A well-known example of this style of production—and one analogous with PC manufacture—is the 19th century watchmaking industry. In England the center of watch production was the city of Coventry, which produced tens of thousands of watches annually, but there was not a single firm that made a complete watch, and there was no firm in the industry with as many as a hundred workers. Incidentally, the phenomenon of networked firms was well understood by Charles Babbage, the pioneer of the computer whose was also a leading economist; Babbage noted of watchmaking in his classic *Economy of Manufactures* (1833) that there were "one hundred and two branches to the art." Coventry business directories of the period list literally hundreds of small firms and sole traders in the watchmaking industry: gear cutters, spring winders, enamellers of dials, case makers, and so on. It was the role of yet another firm, the watch finisher, to assemble the dozens of components that made up the final product; besides the physical assembly of the watch, a major business task was the selection of components, from myriad suppliers, that optimized economy and reliability. With the rise of the large-scale corporation from the 1860s, the various separate branches of the business were gradually absorbed into large, vertically integrated clock- and watchmakers. Much the same happened, on an accelerated scale, in Waltham, Massachusetts, the prominent U.S. watchmaking center.

It should be noted that the old-line computer firms of IBM, NCR, and Burroughs never passed through this industrial transition. At the time they were established, in the period 1870 to 1890, the technology and manufacturing of their early products was relatively undemanding (certainly simpler than making a pocket watch), so that they could be largely self-sufficient. As their products increased in complexity they developed in parallel additional capabilities so that they remained self-sufficient.

Let us now fast forward to 1975 and the beginnings of the PC revolution. The PC was a fantastically complex product, containing a microprocessor, memory and logic chips, a CRT display device, keyboard, and software. No one firm could possibly have all the necessary internal capabilities to manufacture a PC, even a firm as large as IBM. This is where the concept of *external* capabilities comes in.[12] Like the watch finisher of the 1830s, the would-be PC manufacturer had to buy subassemblies from other firms and then integrate them into a saleable product. And as with the watch finisher, proximity to lots of suppliers and rapid informal communications were essential to lubricate the process. This was the Silicon Valley phenomenon.

The best general account of this "modern" form of industrial organization in the IT industry is AnnaLee Saxenian's *Regional Advantage: Culture and Competition in Silicon Valley and Route 128.*[13] Saxenian has identified many of the critical factors that led to the rise of Silicon Valley. Paramount among these are the geographical proximity and the plurality of firms, and the availability of human capital.

Geographical proximity was essential for the whole process to be economically efficient. The PC maker needed to be able to select subassemblies from hundreds of suppliers. In turn, the manufacturers of these subassemblies had to choose from hundreds of component manufacturers; and so on down the supply chain. The geographical proximity of firms, in clusters or networks, reduced transaction costs by making this selection process transparent. In short, a firm could see what it was buying, compare it with a product down the street, and negotiate on price face-to-face. (How much the Internet will eliminate the need for geographical proximity is an open question.)

The second factor, firm plurality, helped to minimize costs though competition. Thus if one wanted to buy a memory board or a memory chip, it was possible to choose from dozens of competing, lean-and-hungry suppliers. Perhaps the only place on earth where both proximity and plurality existed was Silicon Valley. As Saxenian has noted, Route 128—American's other electronics region—was dominated by old-line firms such as IBM, or newer firms such as DEC, that were built on the old vertically integrated model. Along Route 128 there was proximity but not plurality.

Finally, the PC maker—or its supplier—needed human capital in the form of an electronics-savvy workforce. Following the arrival of Frederick Terman at Stanford University in the 1940s, there was a steady output of engineering professionals to feed the electronics industry. These workers were very mobile, drifting from firm to firm, taking their expertise with them. The origin of the Silicon Valley phenomenon in the 1960s has been traced primarily to Fairchild Semiconductor Corporation. It was said that "electronics was in the air" in Silicon Valley during the 1960s and 1970s, and it was one of the few places on earth where two characters such as Apple's Steve Jobs and Steve Wozniak had a good chance of meeting up. While unusually gifted, Jobs and Wozniak were quite typical in their deep informal knowledge of the electronics industry and technology. In the 1980s, other regions of the United States and other countries around the world tried to emulate Silicon Valley. Often it was the lack of human capital and an entrepreneurial culture that caused them to fail to take off in the way anticipated.

Of course, the world moves on, and these factors cannot alone account for the rise of firms such as Intel and Microsoft. These are new giants, quite unlike the old-line firms such as IBM that were one-stop shops for IT goods. They exist primarily as suppliers of components that other, generally much smaller firms integrate into their products. Where these firms fit in the industrial landscape is a question for economic historians of the future.

NOTES

1. Saul Englebourg, *International Business Machines: A Business History* (Harvard University Ph.D. thesis, 1954; reprinted New York: Arno Press, 1976), and Emerson W. Pugh, *Building IBM: Shaping an Industry and Its Technology* (Cambridge, Mass.: MIT Press, 1995).
2. D. Swade, "Babbage to Bill and Way Beyond," *The Times Supplement to Higher Education*, September 12, 1997.
3. Paul Carroll, *Big Blues: The Unmaking of IBM* (New York: Crown Publishers, 1993).

4. Alfred D. Chandler, *The Visible Hand: The Managerial Revolution in American Business* (Cambridge, Mass.: Harvard University Press, 1977), p. 12.
5. James W. Cortada, *Before the Computer: IBM, NCR, Burroughs, and Remington Rand and the Industry They Created, 1865–1956* (Princeton, N.J.: Princeton University Press, 1993).
6. Steven W. Usselman, "IBM and Its Imitators: Organizational Capabilities and the Emergence of the International Computer Industry," *Business and Economic History* 22 (Winter 1993): 1–35.
7. Ibid., p.10.
8. Mark Casson, *Entrepreneurship and Business Culture* (Aldershot, U.K.: Edward Elgar, 1995).
9. John Kao, *Entrepreneurship, Creativity and Organization* (Cambridge, Mass.: Harvard University Press, 1989).
10. Ibid., p. 91.
11. An excellent account of the venture capital industry is William D. Bygrave and Jeffry A. Timmons's *Venture Capital at the Crossroads* (Cambridge, Mass.: Harvard Business School Press, 1992).
12. Richard N. Langlois, "External Economies and Economic Progress: The Case of the Microcomputer Industry," *Business History Review* 66 (Spring, 1992): 1–50.
13. AnnaLee Saxenian, *Regional Advantage: Culture and Competition in Silicon Valley and Route 128* (Cambridge, Mass.: Harvard University Press, 1994).

FOR FURTHER READING

William D. Bygrave and Jeffry A. Timmons, *Venture Capital at the Crossroads* (Cambridge, Mass.: Harvard Business School Press, 1992).
Paul Carroll, *Big Blues: The Unmaking of IBM* (New York: Crown Publishers, 1993).
Mark Casson, *Entrepreneurship and Business Culture* (Aldershot, U.K.: Edward Elgar, 1995).
Alfred D. Chandler, *The Visible Hand: The Managerial Revolution in American Business* (Cambridge, Mass.: Harvard University Press, 1977).
James W. Cortada, *Before the Computer: IBM, NCR, Burroughs, and Remington Rand and the Industry They Created, 1865–1956* (Princeton, N.J.: Princeton University Press, 1993).
Saul Englebourg, *International Business Machines: A Business History* (Ph.D. Dissertation, Harvard University 1954; reprinted New York: Arno Press, 1976).
John Kao, *Entrepreneurship, Creativity and Organization* (Cambridge, Mass.: Harvard University Press, 1989).
Richard N. Langlois, "External Economies and Economic Progress: The Case of the Microcomputer Industry," *Business History Review* 66 (Spring 1992): 1–50.
Emerson W. Pugh, *Building IBM: Shaping an Industry and Its Technology* (Cambridge, Mass.: MIT Press, 1995).

AnnaLee Saxenian, *Regional Advantage: Culture and Competition in Silicon Valley and Route 128* (Cambridge, Mass.: Harvard University Press, 1994).

Steven W. Usselman, "IBM and Its Imitators: Organizational Capabilities and the Emergence of the International Computer Industry," *Business and Economic History* 22 (Winter 1993): 1–35.

15

Government and the Emerging Computer Industry

Robert W. Seidel

In July 1962, I saw my first computer. It was the largest computer in the world: a SAGE computer at Grand Forks Air Force Base. The acronym SAGE stands for Semi-Automatic Ground Environment, which was the first large-scale computer network, built upon the largest of the postwar government projects in computing, Whirlwind at MIT. It was obsolete by the time it was completed, because Soviet Intercontinental Ballistic Missiles replaced the bombers against which it was designed to defend. Nevertheless, to a high-school student, SAGE provided an overwhelming avatar of things to come.

The acronym may also be used to describe the Semi-Automatic Government Environment for scientific and technological development that emerged in the wake of World War II. The military and bureaucratic utility of computers stimulated gigantic investment in them by the government in the era before IBM, and other firms learned how to translate that utility in commercial terms. Much more than the Japanese, British, French, or Soviet governments, the federal government created the modern computer and subsidized its success. The self-made men of Silicon Valley harvested their profits from soil already fertilized and sown by government investment in research, and the history of the early computer industry shows that government support was the critical factor in their development. Although, like interchangeable parts, railroads, aviation, hydroelectric power, and dozens of other technological accomplishments that were nursed to development by the federal government, the computer has been converted in the public mind to a product of the "invisible hand" of the market economy, only ideology and advertising support that view.

Although government support for early technologies was justified as investment in the defense or commerce of America, the Republican Party undertook to subsidize the railroad system of the United States in the era after the Civil War, creating opportunities for "robber barons" to convert public investment into private profit by providing a market for Carnegie's steel and Rockefeller's oil as well as land grants and rate protection for the railroads. The government also provided the human capital and technological knowledge required. The Department of Agriculture, land-grant colleges, and universities established as a result of the Morrill Act of 1862, and the National Bureau of Standards (NBS) engaged in scientific and technological research of direct benefit to industry, just as the Army Signal Corps, Naval Research Laboratory, and Federal armories did for the munitions industry. Military contracts underwrote the innovations in armaments that led to the "American System of Manufactures"—the manufacture of mass-produced items with inter-changeable parts—as well as the development of naval vessels that further enriched the manufacturers of gunpowder and steel. The "visible hand" of government responded to the politics and patronage of the Gilded Era, World War I, and the Roaring Twenties as easily as to the populist and progressive eras of reform that gave a punctuated equilibrium to the evolution of enterprise.

The Colonization of Research

The postwar era colonization of nuclear physics and basic research relating to it in the Atomic Energy Commission (AEC) National Laboratories at Brookhaven, Oak Ridge, and the expansion of conven-tional military research by Office of Naval Research, Air Force, and Army investments in university, industry, and in-house laboratories perma-nently mobilized American science and technology after World War II. In defense of American interests threatened by the Cold War, decolonization of the Third World, and revolutionary movements of all stripes, the federal government expended a sizable fraction of its budget to support high-tech solutions like the atomic and hydrogen bombs, intercontinental ballistic missiles, smart weapons, and radar systems.

The computer was one of the many by-products of this process. While the agencies of the DoD collectively provided most funding for computers, the AEC may have had the largest single-agency budget for computers in the postwar era, reflecting the manifold purposes its scientists had discovered for calculation in the design of nuclear reactors and nuclear weapons. As the sole possessors of the "winning weapon" in the late 1940s, the AEC maintained preferential funding for its laboratories and contractors, who responded by conceiving of capital-intensive solutions to shortages of technical manpower at Los Alamos and other national laboratories. In 1948, Los Alamos Director Norris Bradbury noted that computing had *a more profound effect on the direction of effort of the laboratory in regard to fission weapons* than any postwar program. The shortage of theoretical physicists to design weapons, fissionable material to furnish the nuclear weapons stockpile, and the costs of full-scale tests of nuclear weapons made it more effective to use computer simulations of designs, production processes, and weapon performance whenever possible. The ignition of the hydrogen bomb was simulated in the first program run on the ENIAC in the fall of 1945, and problems related to that device saturated computers for the next 10 years.

The highly technical and highly secret nature of nuclear weapons made political and/or public reform of this system infeasible. Instead, the experts took charge of the stewardship of the nuclear establishment. Laboratory personnel at AEC who rotated in and out of its staff positions in Washington formulated policy and benefited from AEC policy. By their campaign to overturn military control of nuclear weapons, the "atomic scientists" had replaced it not with "civilian control" as the supporters of the McMahon Act—the alternative to the May–Johnson act that prevailed in the postwar struggle for power over atomic energy—believed, but with their own. Wartime power struggles between General Leslie Groves and his scientific prima-donnas was replaced by secret battles between the nuclear barons. The AEC's discrediting of Robert Oppenheimer by Luis Alvarez and Edward Teller was only a tip to this particular iceberg, all the colder because of its immersion in the icy world of physics.

As might be expected, the political agenda of corporate America soon breached the wall of secrecy as effectively as had wartime nuclear spies in the service of the Soviet Union. The Atomic Energy Act of 1954 facilitated nuclear technology transfer to industry just as scientific personnel had already done to academia: Los Alamos scientists transferred much of the technology they developed at Los Alamos during and after World War II. Enrico Fermi, Edward Teller, and Nicolas Metropolis led a hegira to the University of Chicago, which gave up its control of Oak Ridge while retaining Argonne National Laboratory and creating an Institute for Nuclear Studies. Alvarez, Ernest Lawrence, and Edwin McMillan rewarded the University of California for its wartime services by vastly expanding the Radiation Laboratory as well as maintaining Los Alamos, and I. I. Rabi of the General Advisory Committee of the AEC secured a new national laboratory at Brookhaven for Columbia and other northeastern universities.

John von Neumann, a wartime consultant to Los Alamos and to the Army's ENIAC project at University of Pennsylvania, arranged the H-bomb calculation on the ENIAC, and won DoD and AEC support for his computer at the Princeton Institute for Advanced Studies from the AEC in return for AEC rights to copy his computer architecture in their computers at Los Alamos (MANIAC), Argonne (AVIDAC), and Oak Ridge (ORACLE). Los Alamos's MANIAC went into operation before the IAS machine, which was also copied by the Air Force at the RAND Corporation (JOHNNIAC). MANIAC was used to analyze high-energy physics experiments on the Chicago synchocyclotron as well as a wide variety of other scientific experiments, inspiring Alvarez to devise a computer system to analyze data from his liquid hydrogen bubble chamber at the University of California Radiation Laboratory. In 1948, Oak Ridge mathematician Cuthbert Hurd was hired to explore the scientific computer market for IBM. He directed the development of the IBM 701 "Defense Calculator," the IBM 704, and the STRETCH computer, which was designed in collaboration with Los Alamos. The Livermore Branch Radiation Laboratory of the University of California developed the LARC computer with IBM's principal competitor, Sperry-Rand-UNIVAC.

Scientists in the AEC laboratories were discerning and capable users of computers, and interactions with the computer industry provided opportunities to develop computers that were far too expensive to sell to nongovernmental organizations, but incorporated innovations, like transistors, later used in commercial mainframe computers. STRETCH, for example, inspired many of the technological innovations in the IBM 360 series of computers. The AEC laboratories also subsidized the development of supercomputers by firms like Control Data Corporation, Cray Research, and Cray Computer. These machines were the fastest and most powerful computers in the world, reserved for the use of nuclear weapons laboratories, the National Security Agency, and other government clients.

John von Neumann became a member of the AEC's General Advisory Board and subsequently served as an AEC Commissioner, made his IAS machine available for AEC studies of the hydrogen bomb, promoted the development of STRETCH and LARC, and created mechanisms for support of computer research within the AEC. He personified the spirit of this new government agency, run by and for scientists, which had unprecedented authority to control, promote, and develop science and technology. Although the codes used in these machines by the weapons laboratories remained secret, the machines themselves were made available to university users for scientific research, preparing a new generation of computer scientists to train programmers for industrial and commercial use of computers. As in the case of particle accelerators, giant particle detectors, and nuclear reactors, the AEC's sponsorship of computers was turned to the purposes of big science as well as military technology. All of these devices represented the "dual use" philosophy that enhanced recruitment and retention of first-rate scientists by the laboratories of the AEC, while creating a reserve army in case the Cold War became hot.

The Department of Defense and Its Spinoffs

Since the beginning of warfare, scientists have been recruited by soldiers to provide technical expertise. Archimedes at Syracuse, Galileo at the Arsenal of Venice, Leonardo da Vinci in Florence, Lavoisier at the Arsenal in the French Revolution, and Robert Fulton in New York all took up the task of devising instruments of war. This was no less true of computers: Galileo's artillery compass, Charles Babbage's table-making difference engine, and Vannevar Bush's differential analyzer all had military utility and were funded accordingly. The U.S. Army acquired analog computers called "differential analyzers" from Vannevar Bush at MIT to prepare firing tables for artillery in the 1930s. During World War II, the Army not only supported the ENIAC, but also helped to underwrite the development of the Mark I computer by IBM and Harvard. Both of these machines were moved to the Aberdeen Proving Ground after the war, and were supplemented by ORDVAC (Ordnance Variable Automatic Computer), EDVAC (Electronic Discrete Variable Automatic Calculator), and BRLESC (Ballistic Research Laboratory's Electronic Scientific Computer).

Signal lights, semaphores, radio, and telegraph required coded messages, which were particularly important after the German and Japanese navies developed coding and decoding machinery between the World Wars. The Navy, which suffered great losses at Pearl Harbor because of failures in intelligence, set up the CSAW (Communications Special Activity—Washington) to develop devices for cracking enemy codes. The CSAW's devices were special-purpose machines like the British computer Colossus developed by Alan Turing during the war. Many of them were built by the National Cash Register Company in Dayton, Ohio, during the war, and by Engineering Research Associates (ERA), which was founded by CSAW veteran William Norris in 1946.

The Eckert-Mauchly Computer Corporation, like ERA, had subsisted on government contracts while developing computers for commercial use. Both firms were acquired by Remington-Rand in the early 1950s. Remington-Rand also had hired Leslie Groves upon his retirement from the military to run a third facility in Norwalk, Connecticut. When the firm proved incapable of solving the resulting three-body problem, a number of ERA's leading engineers left to found Control Data Corporation (CDC) in 1956. Among them was Seymour Cray, who initiated the Naval Tactical Data System at ERA and afterward became famous for his designs of supercomputers at CDC, Cray Research, and Cray Computer.

The Office of Naval Research (ONR) cast its net broadly in acquiring scientific expertise for the Navy after World War II, in which the Navy had played second fiddle in programs that developed nuclear energy and radar. Eager to underwrite research in fields related to these new devices after the war, ONR supported university research accelerators and computers, like von Neumann's at Princeton and Project Whirlwind at MIT. The Navy's Special Devices Division had originally sponsored MIT's Servomechanisms Laboratory development of a general-purpose flight simulator, but the project's leader, Forrester, had leveraged this support to develop a general-purpose electronic digital computer. Its funding greatly exceeded that of all other ONR computers when it took over the project in the late 1940s, moving the agency to threaten termination of the project. It was rescued from cancellation by the Air Force, which sowed the Whirlwind and reaped SAGE.

The Air Force had a particularly voracious appetite for computing, and SAGE was only one of many systems that the Air Force sponsored for air defense purposes. Even before taking over the Whirlwind project from ONR, the Air Force launched the SCOOP (Scientific Computing for Optimum Problems) to apply techniques like linear programming to its needs. The aerospace industry made frequent use of computers in design and development of planes and guided missiles. For example, in 1946, Northrop Aircraft hired Eckert and Mauchly to design BINAC— a missile guidance computer—for the SNARK missile. Subsequently, the Air Force tasked Bell Labs to develop an all-solid-state digital computer, TRADIC (Transistor Digital Computer), that could be used in an airborne control system, Harvard to build the Mark IV, ERA to build the 1102, General Electric to build OARAC, the University of Michigan to build MIDAC, MIDSAC, and FLAG, Burroughs to build computers to process data for SAGE and the Atlas ICBM's guidance computer, and the National Bureau of Standards to build the NBS Interim computer (SEAC).

The high-tech, hard touch of computers suited DoD agencies' requirements for real-time systems that could defend against attacks by aircraft, and for data-processing systems that could provide logistical support for military units from Germany to Korea, just as the AEC found computers a useful substitute for theoretical physicists, mathematicians, and human "computers" in designing nuclear weapons, reactors, and production processes. These martial machines, however, were for all practical purposes indistinguishable from their civil counterparts, which were promoted by the National Bureau of Standards.

The NBS and the Computer Business

The NBS was headed by another patron of computing, Edward U. Condon, a theoretical physicist and research manager whose calculation of the tunnel effect in quantum mechanics—in which a charged particle penetrates the nucleus of an atom without exceeding the Coulomb potential surrounding it—inspired the first successful atom-smashing particle accelerators in the 1930s. Like his subatomic bullets, the NBS overcame potential barriers to technology transfer to government computer projects outside the realm of military computing. As the government's principal civilian R&D facility, it fell to them to standardize computer technology through specifying performance requirements in the large government market and to negotiate with the computer industry to provide computers for government agencies.

In addition to providing specifications and conducting negotiations for government computers, the NBS was responsible for the planning, design, and fabrication of prototype computers. This was the result of its prewar experience in calculating in the Mathematical Tables Project, and the interest of other agencies, like the Bureau of the Census, in acquiring electronic digital computers before they were commercially available. In 1947, it asked the NBS to select a contractor and to oversee its construction of a computer for the 1950 census. The Air Force subsequently requested that the NBS oversee a crash development program for an electronic digital computer, the NBS Interim Computer, later renamed SEAC (Standards Eastern Electronic Computer). The SEAC went into operation in April 1950, and was followed by SWAC (Standards Western Electronic Computer). The NBS also designed the DYSEAC, one of the first transportable digital computers. The NBS also collected, publicized, and disseminated technical information, studied the application of computers to government agency problems, including patent indexing, mail processing, radioactive fallout prediction, savings bond processing, Social Security wage record keeping, and systems for payroll processing, cost accounting, and statistical and financial reports. The NBS supported the paperwork task force, or "Hoover Commission" study, which revealed that the federal government processed 25 billion individual pieces of paper annually, including 240 million wage records, 400 million checks, three-quarters of a million savings bonds, 300 million postal money orders, payroll and millions of items in the military supply and logistics inventory.

The Bureau set up an elaborate institutional structure to provide the research and development required by its suzerainty over government computing: the National Applied Mathematical Laboratories (NAML) and Institute for Numerical Analysis (INA) in Los Angeles, and the Computation Laboratory, Statistical Engineering Laboratory, and Machine Development Laboratory in Washington. An Applied Mathematics Panel including von Neumann, Mina Rees of the Office of Naval Research, and Edward Teller of the University of Chicago oversaw their activity. Department of Defense agencies provided over 75% of NAML funding from 1947 to 1953 and the AEC took over SEAC for a year to perform the extensive calculations required to design the hydrogen bomb. Scientists from AEC replaced INA staff to ensure security. When the Secretary of Defense decided to move such applied scientific work for the DoD back into their laboratories, the resulting NBS budget cuts forced NAML's closing. Condon himself was hounded from office by the Red Scare of the early 1950s, and the NBS lost its grip on government computing standards.

The NSF and University Computing

The NBS's role in academic computing was gradually assumed by the National Science Foundation (NSF) which was formally established by Congress in 1950. The NSF's discipline-oriented program funded projects in physics, chemistry, and other sciences. When asked to support computers, the NSF turned to the NBS for advice. After NAML was disestablished, the NSF surveyed applied mathematics in the United States. The survey found that many natural and social scientists were making increased use of computational techniques. In particular they noted that large scientific facilities like accelerators, nuclear reactors, and mainframe computers were used by many inter- and multidisciplinary groups. The NSF funded von Neumann's work at Princeton, and von Neumann persuaded NSF's overseer, the National Science Board, to fund computers for astronomy, physics, and chemistry. Although modest until

1958, the NSF program increased its grants in reaction to Sputnik, providing $200,000 to three universities in 1958, funded the acquisition of computers by 18 schools in 1959. In 1969, the Mathematical, Physical, and Engineering Division forecast computer costs of $10,000,000 per year in 1962, and $31–70 million thereafter. Congress authorized NSF support of computing facilties in 1961, and such support increased from $2.5 to $11.3 million annually between 1961 and 1967.

During this period, defense and space spending for research also increased, and DoD and its spinoff, the National Aeronautics and Space Administration (NASA) reacted to university attempts to provide "free time" for researchers by "taxing" contracts by convincing the Office of Management and Budget to impose a uniform rate for all users. Despite its desire to provide "unfettered" research, the NSF had to avoid conflict between other agencies' contract research and its grants, since overcharging by computer centers to contracts had been detected by auditors, and agreed to the provision of less "free computer time." President Lyndon Johnson's efforts to expand the distribution of research funding to previously neglected regions led the NSF to create a regional computing program administered by a new Office of Computing Activities (OCA), which coordinated all of the NSF's computing programs and created 30 regional computing centers serving 350 schools. John Pasta, the former head of the AEC computing program, presided over a consolidation and reduction of the NSF computing program in 1973, dismantling the OCA into the Division of Computer Research, while the Directorate for Science Education took over all of OCA's functions related to education. The Division of Computer Research subsequently merged with the Mathematics Section of NSF to form the Division of Mathematical and Computer Sciences, which strengthened support for computer science and engineering research.

In the late 1950s, IBM was a pioneer in equipping universities with computers, supplying many universities with IBM 1401 computers at educational discounts, and NSF continued that trend in its facilities programs. The termination of these programs left many smaller schools without the access to computing facilities that they had enjoyed in the 1960s, as larger universities absorbed regional centers or charged prohibitive fees for computer time. Between 1967 and 1976, federal funding for scientific facilities like computers fell by more than half, and federal support for academic research in computing declined from the high levels of the preceding decade. Money poured instead into the Department of Defense, which, in response to Congressional directives like the Mansfield Amendment, shifted its research funds to its own laboratories and industry. This marginalized the "butter" promised under

Lyndon B. Johnson's Great Society programs in order to build more guns for Vietnam. In particular, classified research for DoD and AEC programs shifted from universities for federally funded research and development centers as students protested the prostitution of academia by the Pentagon. The costs and declining support for the war further restricted universities' funding for research and computing, until the situation became sufficiently threatening that the NSF stepped in to create regional supercomputing facilities in 1985.

NASA

The National Aeronautics and Space Administration (NASA) sprang from the brow of the Department of Defense in 1958, in reaction to Sputnik and scientific advisors who found the military space effort wanting. It incorporated the National Advisory Committee on Aeronautics, which had funded civilian and military aircraft research from 1915 onward. Because space flight required complex command and control, NASA became a major procurer of computer equipment. Its fifth largest contractor was IBM, followed by Sperry-Rand (17th), Honeywell (21st), Computer Science Corporation (27th) Control Data Corporation (42nd), and a number of smaller firms. Like the DoD, NASA favored extramural contract research managed by intramural laboratories. It developed miniaturized computer systems and large computer networks. Together with DoD missile programs, the space program drove the development of the integrated circuit from primitive models to very large scale integrated systems. The integrated circuit revolutionized computer design, making possible minicomputers as well as microcomputers. The first minicomputer, the Digital Equipment Corporation's PDP-1, was a spinoff of the SAGE project, while the first microcomputers were built by hobbyists using integrated circuits like the Intel 8080, introduced in 1984.

DARPA

The space race produced another significant agency to support computer research and development: the Defense Advanced Research Projects Agency (DARPA). Founded in 1958 in the wake of the Soviet Union's loss of Sputnik, DARPA promoted the kind of leading-edge research that the services could not support. Its Information Processing Techniques Office (IPTO) was responsible for sponsoring the development of many of the technological components of today's Information Age, from the mouse to the Internet, and provided more support for computing than any other federal agency by the 1970s, as other chapters in this volume demonstrate (e.g., chapters 10 and 11).

The agency eliminated the NSF peer review process and streamlined the DoD contract process in order to facilitate rapid development of military computer systems for command and control, exotic antimissile radar systems, and many other military processes. Like the early AEC programs, IPTO was dominated by university computer scientists who rotated between the agency and universities, provoking one defense administrator to complain that science was the only pork barrel in which the pigs divided the pork. And, like the AEC and the ONR, which had generously funded research without too many scruples about military application, IPTO drew upon the best and the brightest scientists in academia and industry, offering autonomy in exchange for expertise, and funding in exchange for unfettered research. As in its other programs to develop lasers, precision-guided munitions, and automated battlefield systems, DARPA enjoyed great freedom to cultivate its academic and industrial clients with a Medician patronage.

Regulation

Although it lavished support and subsidies for research, the federal government used its regulatory powers to prevent single firms from dominating the computer industry that benefited from them. The most famous of these interventions was *United States v. International Business Machines Corporation* (U.S. District Court, 69 Civ. 200 [DNE]), one of the largest antitrust cases to be brought to trial in the United States, on May 19, 1975. The government charged IBM with monopolizing the market for general-purpose digital computers, systems, and markets for peripherals in violation of section 2 of the Sherman Act. The government abandoned the lawsuit in January, 1982, after IBM "unbundled" its software from computers, without conceding monopoly practices.

Other regulatory arms of the government have also impinged on the industry. The Federal Communications Commission regulated computer emissions of radio-frequency signals, whether intended or unintended, to protect commercial and amateur broadcasters. Export control laws have limited dissemination of state-of-the art computers, especially super-computers of the kind used for weapons design in the AEC laboratories. Although this regulation does not differ in kind from that of other technologies, the rapid advances in computer technology have certainly led to many more opportunities for litigation than in most other industries.

Conclusion

"Government" is the "visible hand" in the computer industry. It contributed to the development of the computer industry through its civilian and military procurement programs, and was the only customer of the industry capable of influencing suppliers through its standards, its research and development funds, and its specifications for high-performance computing, as well as its regulatory power. Most of the early computers sold by the industry went to government agencies, and the adoption of the von Neumann architecture reflected the interest of IBM and other manufacturers in replacing machines originally built by government with computers, like the 701 "defense calculator" that did the same jobs in the same way. The construction of LARC, STRETCH, and the CDC high-performance computers, as well as the UNIVAC I's for government markets also made government-stimulated innovation central to the development of computers.

The commercial market, on the other hand, did not provide an effective demand for the electronic digital computer until the government had "picked winners" among industrial firms, and demonstrated their efficacy in functions long dominated by punch card calculators and other business machines. As IBM's rise to market dominance testifies, success in meeting government specifications translated into success in the commercial marketplace. As the midwife of the computing industry, the government made it possible to emerge from the womb of war to the world of peace.

The emergence of the computing industry under government patronage created an environment that favored the development of the minicomputers and microcomputers that gradually came to replace the mainframe computers that embellished the giant government computer facilities. The personal computer became a commodity within a few years after its invention, and, by the end of the century, the Internet, having been reinvented as the World Wide Web, provided a rapidly growing communications environment within which the PC flourished. It became possible for a Presidential candidate to take credit for inventing the Internet, and for computer firms to produce machines far more powerful and far less expensive than their predecessors, to which they bore the same relationship as lizards do to chameleons. Now, rather than olive green or navy blue, computers are multicolored, and multipurpose, and they multiply much faster than their martial ancestors. It cannot be said that computing would not have emerged without the intervention of the federal government. The emerging computer industry, however, could not have developed without government patronage, which supplied the market and means for its development.

FOR FURTHER READING

William Aspray and Bernard O. Williams, "Arming American Scientists: NSF and the Provision of Scientific Computing Facilities for Universities, 1950–1973," *IEEE Annals of the History of Computing* 16/4 (Winter 1994): 60–74.

Paul E. Ceruzzi, *Beyond the Limits: Flight Enters the Computer Age* (Cambridge, Mass.: MIT Press, 1989).

Paul N. Edwards, *The Closed World: Computers and the Politics of Discourse in Cold War America* (Cambridge, Mass.: MIT Press, 1996).

Kenneth Flamm, *Creating the Computer: Government, Industry, and High Technology* (Washington, D.C.: Brookings Institution, 1988).

Shane M. Greenstein, "Lock-in and the Costs of Switching Mainframe Computer Vendors in the US Federal Government in the 1970s," *IEEE Annals of the History of Computing* 17 (Fall 1995): 58–66.

Arthur L. Norberg, "High-technology Calculation in the Early 20th Century: Punched Card Machinery in Business and Government," *Technology and Culture* 31 (1990): 753–779.

Arthur L. Norberg, et al., *Transforming Computer Technology: Information Processing for the Pentagon, 1962–1986* (Baltimore: Johns Hopkins University Press, 1995).

Robert W. Seidel, " 'Crunching Numbers': Computers and Physical Research in the AEC Laboratories," *History and Technology* 15 (1998): 31–68.

The History of Computing Literature

James W. Cortada

There now exists a growing body of general histories and specialized monographs on the history of computing that makes it possible to understand the main outlines of the story. Two important general histories set the stage. Martin Campbell-Kelly and William Aspray, *Computer: A History of the Information Machine* (New York: Basic Books, 1996) is a detailed but general history of the subject. For an overview that emphasizes technical developments, see Paul Ceruzzi, *A History of Modern Computing* (Cambridge, Mass.: MIT Press, 1998). The most useful photographic essay on the subject is by C. Eames and R. Eames, *A Computer Perspective: Background to the Computer Age* (Cambridge, Mass.: Harvard University Press, 1990).

On the period prior to the arrival of the computer, William Aspray, ed., *Computing Before Computers* (Ames, Iowa: Iowa State University Press, 1990) offers a group of chapters written by historians. For a history of the information industry in the United States prior to the computer, see James W. Cortada, *Before the Computer: IBM, NCR, Burroughs, and Remington Rand and the Industry They Created, 1865–1956* (Princeton, N.J.: Princeton University Press, 1993). JoAnne Yates wrote a book on how information was managed and used in corporations in the late 19th and early 20th century through a series of case studies, *Control Through Communication: The Rise of System in American Management* (Baltimore, Md.: Johns Hopkins University Press, 1989). For a study of the role of information in general in American organizations in the same period see

James R. Beniger, *The Control Revolution: Technological and Economic Origins of the Information Society* (Cambridge, Mass.: Harvard University Press, 1986). Two books discuss the role of information and their technologies across several centuries: Alfred D. Chandler, Jr. and James W. Cortada (eds.), *A Nation Transformed by Information: How Information Has Shaped the United States from Colonial Times to the Present* (New York: Oxford University Press, 2000), and James W. Cortada, *Making the Information Society: Experience, Consequences and Possibilities* (Upper Saddle River, N.J.: Financial Times/Prentice Hall, 2002).

There is a very large collection of books on the history of computer technology. On the ENIAC we now have Scott McCartney, *ENIAC: The Triumphs and Tragedies of the World's First Computer* (New York: Walker and Company, 1999). For a useful history of the transistor see Michael Riordan and Lillian Hoddeson, *Crystal Fire: The Invention of the Transistor and the Birth of the Information Age* (New York: W.W. Norton, 1997). Two books do an excellent job in describing the role of the U.S. government in launching the computer age: Kenneth Flamm, *Creating the Computer: Government, Industry, and High Technology* (Washington, D.C.: The Brookings Institution, 1988) and Paul N. Edwards, *The Closed World: Computers and the Politics of Discourse in Cold War America* (Cambridge, Mass.: MIT Press, 1996). A difficult book to get, but worth the hunt, is Stan Augarten, *Bit by Bit: An Illustrated History of Computers* (New York: Ticknor & Fields, 1984).

While there are less-thorough histories of software, see the collection of essays, many by software developers, Thomas M. Bergin and Richard G. Gibson, eds., *History of Programming Languages II* (New York: ACM Press, 1996). See also Paul W. Oman and Ted G. Lewis, eds., *Milestones in Software Evolution* (Los Alamitos, Calif.: IEEE Computer Society Press, 1990). Finally, there is the massive set of essays in Richard Wexelblat, ed., *History of Programming Languages* (New York: Academic Press, 1981). For memoirs, see Robert Glass, *In the Beginning: Recollections of Software Pioneers* (Los Alamitos, Calif.: IEEE Computer Society, 1998). We do not yet have a comprehensive history of PC software. However, for an introduction see Forrest Mims, III, *Siliconnections: Coming of Age in the Electronic Era* (New York: McGraw-Hill, 1986).

On the PC, there is a growing body of company and machine histories. On Apple Computer, see Lee Butcher, *The Rise and Fall of Steve Jobs at Apple Computer* (New York: Paragon House, 1987) and Jim Carlton, *Apple: The Inside Story of Intrigue, Egomania, and Business Blunders* (New York: Times Business, 1997). On IBM's role see James Chposky and Ted Leonsis, *Blue Magic: The People, Power and Politics Behind the IBM Personal Computer* (New York: Facts on File, 1988).

Microsoft has been the subject of numerous books; perhaps the most useful of the lot is by Michael A. Cusumano and Richard W. Selby, *Microsoft Secrets: How the World's Most Powerful Software Company Creates Technology, Shapes Markets, and Manages People* (New York: Free Press, 1995). On the Internet, see Katie Hafner and Matthew Lyon, *Where Wizards Stay Up Late: The Origins of the Internet* (New York: Simon & Schuster, 1996) and for a more detailed history on its origins, there is Arthur L. Norberg and Judy E. O'Neill, *Transforming Computer Technology: Information Processing for the Pentagon, 1962–1986* (Baltimore, Md.: Johns Hopkins University Press, 1996). For an excellent history of the PC and its software, there is Paul Freibergh and Michael Swaine, *Fire in the Valley: The Making of the Personal Computer* (New York: McGraw-Hill, 2nd ed., 1999).

Histories of the information-processing industry explain how this technology was brought to market, sold, and constantly replaced with new products. Martin Campbell-Kelly wrote a history that explains events in Great Britain, *ICL: A Business and Technical History* (Oxford: Clarendon Press, 1989), while a detailed economic history explains early U.S. developments: Franklin M. Fisher, James W. McKie, and Richard B. Mancke, *IBM and the U.S. Data Processing Industry: An Economic History* (New York: Praeger, 1983) and Emerson W. Pugh, *Building IBM: Shaping an Industry and Its Technology* (Cambridge, Mass.: MIT Press, 1995), now the best single volume available on IBM. For a major new business history of the industry, see Alfred D. Chandler, Jr., *Inventing the Electronic Century: The Epic Story of the Consumer Electronics and Computer Industry* (New York: Free Press, 2001). For an excellent account of how two American regions became computing centers see AnnaLee Saxenian, *Regional Advantage: Culture and Competition in Silicon Valley and Route 128* (Cambridge, Mass.: MIT Press, 1995).

There are a number of guides to the literature and archives on computing's history. On archives there is a little book of essays written by archivists, James W. Cortada, ed., *Archives of Data-Processing History: A Guide to Major U.S. Collections* (Westport, Conn.: Greenwood Press, 1990). The leading archival center on computing is the Charles Babbage Institute (CBI) at the University of Minnesota, which periodically publishes finding aids and posts material to its web site. Keeping current on what is being published is a challenge because so much is now coming into print. Begin with CBI's Newsletter, which provides a small bibliography of recently published articles and books in each issue. Then go to the journal that publishes the most on the history of computing, and always includes a bibliography and book reviews, memoirs and news on the history of information processing, the *IEEE Annals of the History of Computing.* It also reports on bibliographies and historical dictionaries published on the history of computing. For an introduction to sources on the Internet, see Dennis A. Trinkle, et al., *The History Highway: A Guide to Internet Resources* (Armonk, N.Y.: M.E. Sharpe, 1997).

Archives and
Online Sources

Henry Lowood

It is important to keep in mind that there are hundreds, if not thousands, of archival repositories and online resources with collections that are relevant, at least in part, to the history of computers and computing. Consider topics such as the history of hospital information management, library database technology, scientific computation, digital typography, or computer graphics in the film industry. Many kinds of institutions have produced significant historical records, and, in turn, these records may be found in many different kinds of repositories, from relatively open government record centers and university archives to relatively closed private collections and corporate records centers. The spectrum ranges from the Library of Congress to the Disney archives.

Archives

In the United States, the development of archival collections in the history of computing resembles other areas of postwar documentation in the history of science, technology, and medicine. The common factor is the massive expansion of activity in technoscientific fields of every ilk, especially in programs tied to federal and military funding, large-scale projects, or areas of intense industrial or commercial development. In each case, besides merely changing all of our lives fundamentally, these activities have stimulated the evolution of new institutions that rely on or provide funding and support for research and development. These include governmental funding agencies, national laboratories, industrial organizations and research laboratories, technology licensing offices in universities, and independent think-tanks. A many-fold increase in the production of records has resulted from the rapid expansion of technoscience in our society and the growth of these institutions.

In fields of activity closely tied to computers and computing, the growth of the archival record has been multifaceted. Obviously, the production of records continues unabated. There is very little to say about this evident fact, except that it has had and will continue to have enormous implications for the capacity of existing repositories to document recent and contemporary computing. Also, the advance of computer-related research, technology, applications, and uses, as well as the institutions that support research and development, have led to new forms or increasingly complicated systems of records; some examples are grant applications, semipublished technical reports arising from funded projects, legal documentation—patents, copyright, antitrust law, ergonomics, privacy, and so on are legal issues related in various ways to computing—reports to shareholders, and the lobbying records of trade associations. Finally, the diversity of formats of historical records existing today is unprecedented, with a rate of change that appears to be increasing. The transition from paper to electronic forms of record storage and the proliferation of video and digital media both have enormous implications for archival programs, for example.

Archives are preserved records of the activities of organizations or individuals. A narrower understanding of this term is limited to departments responsible for historical records of enduring value in a larger organization of which they are a part; examples are the Hewlett-Packard Archives or IBM Archives. Note that such archives may or may not be found in the same part of the organizational chart as records managers responsible for current records, retention schedules, and the like. In other words, documents of potential historical value do not necessarily reside in archives. With the widespread acquisition of historical records by hundreds, if not thousands, of archival repositories and special collections units of libraries (often called manuscript collections) in the United States alone, the term "archives" is expanding to mean documents themselves, often as shorthand for manuscript collections, personal papers, collections of historical documentation in a particular field, or even, unpublished materials. These materials may end up on the shelves of a collector, a library, or a disciplinary history center. At issue here is whether we think of archives simply as any collections of historical records or as necessarily arising out of and being preserved within the institutional context of their creation.

Of course, the records of individuals and institutions are often, if not usually, dispersed, discarded, weeded, or lost. Many migration patterns are possible: entire archives may be transferred to or acquired by repositories with no organic connection to their original site of creation; the files of distinct laboratories or projects may end up in the garage of a lab director or principle investigator; the personal papers of important researchers may be acquired by libraries, historical societies, or disciplinary historical centers; and individual documents may end up in museums or private collections, to name only a few possibilities.

Permutations and combinations of these scenarios abound the records of Burroughs Corporation, originally held in the Burroughs and then in the Unisys corporate archives, are now at the Charles Babbage Institute at the University of Minnesota; series of records from Sperry-UNIVAC can be found at The Hagley Museum and Library in Wilmington, Delaware, as the result of acquisitions that included large collections of documentation created as a result of patent infringement litigation; the surviving records of the Augmentation Research Center at the Stanford Research Institute (now SRI International) were acquired by the Department of Special Collections at Stanford with the personal papers of Douglas C. Engelbart from McDonnell-Douglas Information Systems, which had acquired Tymshare Corporation, which had earlier acquired the project from the Stanford Research Institute; and so on. It is important that, even in the case of a large, active organization or a prominent individual associated with a particular institution, records can be scattered to distant repositories. Incidentally, even though libraries and archives typically distinguish between organizational records and personal papers of individuals, the Engelbart example reminds us that these two categories are often permeable, something to keep in mind when you are hunting for archival collections.

So, where are the collections? *Archives of Data-Processing History* provides a good overview of the major repositories in the field, even though many collections have been made available since 1990. A recent list of "archives specializing in the history of computing," prepared by Bruce Bruemmer for *History of Programming Languages II*, published by the ACM, updates contact information found in *Archives of Data-Processing History*, but otherwise the roster of important archival institutions remained generally unchanged in the 1990s. This core group of archives consists of the Charles Babbage Institute, the Computer Museum, the Hagley Museum and Library, the Library of Congress, the

National Archives and Records Administration, the Smithsonian Institution, and the Stanford University Libraries, plus several corporate archives (IBM, AT&T, Texas Instruments, etc.). Other significant collections located in university libraries or archives can be found at Dartmouth, Harvard, MIT, Carnegie-Mellon, Illinois, and Pennsylvania. A few independent museums of computing have been founded since 1990, and both Microsoft and Intel are establishing archives or museums. In all, there are fewer than 10 institutions in the United States that actively collect research materials in the history of computing; another dozen or more feature important, but generally static collections or limit the scope of their collecting to the mission of institutional archives in the narrow sense.

And yet, countless institutions offer potentially relevant materials, so that finding historical records in the history of computing, as in many other areas, usually involves two mindsets. On the one hand, you should invest time to understand the resources available in the major repositories and centers focused on the history of computing, where book and reference collections, knowledgeable staff, and other support materials can inform and refine your search for sources on a specific topic. On the other, you will need to learn to use printed and online guides and databases to locate archival sources in repositories that have not specialized in the history of computing and may not be equipped to describe or interpret what they have in detail.

Online Sources and Other Electronic Resources

Archives and historical writing both respond to a societal need to preserve cultural memory. Archivists and historians concerned with the history of computing in the 1990s realize that most cultural records produced today are created and stored in digital form. At the same time, archivists are not yet entirely comfortable with digital media, despite considerable attention on the difficulties they present and detailed knowledge of the obstacles to reliable archival preservation of electronic media. As one recent report put it, the essential problem is that "reading and understanding information in digital form requires equipment and software, which is changing constantly and may not be available within a decade of its introduction" (*Preserving Digital Information*, 2).

Clearly, problems remain to be solved before information preserved only in digital form can be considered archival resources as traditionally understood by historians. Yet, from the standpoint of writing history of computing, especially recent computing, electronic media are fast catching up with paper libraries and archives as indispensable sources of information. Also, information tools for archival control or bibliographic searching have become fixtures of historical research. The availability of these tools, combined with intensifying interest in reliable preservation of online sources and the explosive growth of the Internet and World Wide Web promises to transform the use of source materials by historians of computing, as indeed, for historians of every sort.

It may be useful to divide online sources into three categories. First, *traditional electronic resources* arose out of printed bibliographies, card catalogs, and multivolume union catalogs, such as the National Union Catalog of Printed Books (NUC) and National Union Catalog of Manuscript Collections (NUCMUC). Beginning in the 1960s, when the Library of Congress began to make their catalog records available not only in printed, but also in machine-readable form, library automation has led to the creation of standards and systems for bibliographic information. The MARC ("machine-readable cataloging") record format, completed in 1968, created a basis for the communication of this information, and it is now the foundation for virtually every American online bibliographic catalog. In the 1970s, related standards were approved by the International Organization for Standardization (ISO) and American National Standards Institute (ANSI), so that there are now many national MARC standards. Formats have been developed for books, serials, maps, and other information formats, including archives and manuscripts with the adoption of the MARC-AMC (Archives, Manuscripts, and Control format). For several years now, the digital equivalents of NUC and NUCMUC—only much larger and with enhanced access and searching—have been available through bibliographic utilities such as OCLC and RLIN.

What this all means is that catalog information is now readily exchanged among libraries and databases. With the implementation of a new generation of online library catalogs based on hypermedia and web technology, the day is fast approaching when integrated searching of a configurable suite of databases, catalogs, and indexes—many with cataloging based on current library standards and shared authority databases for controlled fields, names, geographical places, and the like—will be available from a scholar's desktop. A good place to search for library information is an Internet resources page provided by a research library, such as the "Catalogs from Other Libraries" page provided by Northwestern University: <http://www.library.northwestern.edu/catalogs/index.html>. Specialized subject bibliographies with citations to articles and other publications in the history of computing are among the most important online resources available from the scholar's computer desktop. Foremost among them, the History of Science and Technology File from the Research Libraries Group can be used via local online catalogs, RLIN and the World Wide Web; this database combines the online versions of a growing set of annual and current bibliographies in the history of science and technology. Many other bibliographic files devoted to computer science and electrical engineering are widely available and include references to historical articles. Librarians are the best source of information about these resources and their availability.

Second, *independent sources of information* created for the Internet and, specifically, the World Wide Web have opened up new avenues for the dissemination of primary sources, online publication of historical studies, group discussion, and the exchange of information. Indeed, the web has opened up access to a variety of formats and sources that previously would only have been available via personal contact. Online publications, discussion lists and bulletin boards, private homepages, guides and frequently-asked-question lists, compilations of links to other sites, and topical sites all gather resources, most of them not readily available or even conceivable in print, for ready use. The web is a computer-based medium, after all, and therefore it should be no surprise that much of this information is connected with a wide range of interests in the history of computing. Indeed, one of the great benefits of the availability of resources via the web is that it has opened up access to previously ephemeral, unpublished, or local resources, such as filmed document-aries and interviews, newsletters, museum holdings, and private collections.

Corporate and some government sites also fall into this category. Web pages created by private companies and corporations frequently offer company histories or timelines as "extras," corporate back-grounders, investor information, or interviews and other background material about technology, corporate structure, industrial organizations, or executives and founders of companies. These pages provide, incidentally, a good place to look for information about corporate archives, libraries, and museums, both real and virtual. The Virtual Museum of Computing <http://www.comlab.ox.ac.uk/archive/other/museums/computing.html> on the web offers a useful list of corporate histories, computing organizations, online museums, and other links to sites in all of these categories. Most of the major archival organizations in the United States and in many other countries maintain useful websites with contact information and, in some cases, detailed information about holdings.

Third, *digital libraries and archives* are collections of online documents consisting not just of bibliographic information, but of the sources themselves. They are maintained for use, delivery, or preservation by organizations capable of continuing this responsibility for the long term and following a set of agreed-upon professional and technical standards (such as MARC) to do so. The Digital Collections Inventory Report <http://www.clir.org/pubs/reports/mcclung/>, sponsored by the Commission on Preservation and Access and the Council on Library Resources, presents the results of an inventory conducted during the second half of 1995. The list, available over the web, describes and provides links to many such projects and gives an overview of the different approaches to creating and providing access to large-scale digital collections.

Today, few projects merely scan published or unpublished materials for delivery as images. Current projects include provisions for the creation and searching of metadata (such as cataloging information); links between catalogs, finding aids and other indexes, on the one hand, and a collection of authorized and carefully maintained documents on the other; and attention to issues of long-term preservation and migration of data. They may take the form of image databases with associated metadata; searchable electronic text collections (whether generated from scanned images or entered manually), or full-blown "text encoding" projects involving textual mark-up using the Standard Generalized Markup Language (SGML) or Hypertext Markup Language (HTML). In the archival realm, careful attention has been given to opening up the multiple levels of descriptive information available through archival finding aids by encoding and making them available on websites, often with links to either online catalogs or electronic documents.

Digital conversion projects and the preservation of original electronic archives of information created and stored only in electronic form are two paths toward the creation of substantial digital collections. The next steps in defining digital libraries and archives will integrate techniques for producing and preserving collections; web technology for browsing, linking, and searching; and a commitment to the established library and archival standards and practices to locate, authenticate, control, and provide access to source materials, whether publications, archives, or their digital equivalents. Digital archives, for example, will integrate finding aids that describe the contents of archival collections; local and union databases of catalog records for archives based on the AMC format; citation and authority files with related information; images of archival documents, with SGML- or HTML-encoded databases searchable by text or metadata provided according to emerging standards. As these large collections of resources begin to populate the computer-based networks that are, increasingly, a part of our research lives, the notion of digital libraries and archives as vast storehouses of information akin to their physical counterparts—as real themselves and not merely virtual—will eventually be realized.

FOR FURTHER READING

Bruce Bruemmer and Sheldon Hochheiser, *The High Technology Company* (Minneapolis, Minn.: Charles Babbage Institute, The Center for the History of Information Processing, University of Minnesota, 1989).

Michael Nash, *Computers, Automation, and Cybernetics at the Hagley Museum and Library* (Wilmington, Del.: Hagley Museum and Library, 1989).

Michael R. Williams, "Preserving Britain's Computer Heritage: The National Archive for the History of Computing," *Annals of the History of Computing* 11 (1989): 313–319.

Michael R. Williams, ed., "Museums and Archives," *Annals of the History of Computing* 10 (1989): 305–329.

REFERENCES

Bruce H. Bruemmer, *Resources for the History of Computing: A Guide to U.S. and Canadian Records,* with the assistance of Thomas Traub and Celeste Brosenne (Minneapolis, Minn.: Charles Babbage Institute, The Center for the History of Information Processing, University of Minnesota, 1987).

James W. Cortada, *Archives of Data-Processing History: A Guide to Major U.S. Collections* (New York: Greenwood, 1990).

Patricia A. McClung, "Digital Collections Inventory Report" (February 1996): <http://www.clir.org/pubs/reports/mcclung/>.

Preserving Digital Information: Report of the Task Force on Archiving of Digital Information (Washington, D.C.: Commission on Preservation and Access, 1996).

Oral History

Frederik Nebeker

In the 19th century, as historical scholarship found a place at most European universities, there was established what is called the documentary tradition in history. It required that the historian cite all sources and use, as sources, only original documents. A standard introduction to the study of history published near the end of that century opened with the unqualified statement "The historian works with documents.... There is no substitute for documents: no documents, no history." The documentary tradition remains strong in academic history today, and the abundant use of oral evidence makes an account seem to be journalism rather than history.

Yet historians from ancient Greece to the present have frequently needed to rely on oral evidence in order to give a full account of events. Herodotus and Thucydides, for example, compared the accounts given by different eyewitnesses to the same events. In the eighth century the Anglo-Saxon scholar Bede, in his *History of the English Church and People*, used both documentary sources and oral evidence, commenting at one point, "I am not dependent on any one author, but on countless faithful *witnesses* who either know or remember the facts." And leading historians of the 19th century, such as Jules Michelet and Thomas Macaulay, made much use of oral testimony.

Technological advance in the mid-20th century has made it easier to draw on personal recollections without subverting the documentary tradition: by recording the recollections on tape, transcribing the tape, and making the tape publicly accessible, this evidence becomes part of the documentary record. These taped interviews are often called oral history, and since the 1960s they have been produced in large numbers.

Several factors help explain the recent rise to prominence of oral history. There has been a great deal of interest in types of history—social history, the history of everyday life, labor history, women's history, rural history—for which documents are often unavailable or scant. In earlier periods, diaries and correspondence recorded many events as well as the thoughts, feelings, and motivations of the actors; such written records are much less common today, in part because of new forms of communication, notably the telephone and email. There is also the greater feasibility of oral history: inexpensive, portable cassette tape recorders became available in the mid-1960s, in the same decade that oral history rose to prominence. The result of these and other factors is that today at colleges and universities oral history is taught as a part of historical method.

The historiography of computing has been enriched by numerous oral-history programs and projects. There exists one guide: Center for the History of Electrical Engineering, *Sources in Electrical History 2: Oral History Collections in U.S. Repositories* (New Brunswick, N.J.: IEEE Center for the History of Electrical Engineering, 1992). It summarizes the contents of more than 1000 interviews stored in 64 different repositories. Many of these interviews were created in large oral-history projects, and 57 such projects are described in this guide.

Two discipline-history centers—the Charles Babbage Institute and the IEEE History Center—and the Smithsonian Institution are responsible for a large part of the existing oral histories dealing with computers.

The richest collection of interviews on the history of computing is at the Charles Babbage Institute at the University of Minnesota. Some 300 interviews include ones with Gene Amdahl, John Atanasoff, Arthur Burks, J. Presper Eckert, Herman Goldstine, Grace Hopper, John Mauchly, Marvin Minsky, Ivan Sutherland, and Konrad Zuse.

The IEEE History Center at Rutgers University has a continuing oral-history program aimed at illuminating the recent history of all electrical and computing technologies. A substantial part of the more than 350 interviews in the Center's collection concern the history of computing. There are, for example, interviews with Thelma Estrin, Federico Faggin, Edwin Harder, William Hewlett, Albert S. Hoagland, John McPherson, Jan Rajchman, and Erwin Tomash.

Another discipline-history center, the Center for History of Physics of the American Institute of Physics (AIP), holds a very large oral-history collection, and many of the interviews deal with computer history. For example, Vannevar Bush and John Kemeny are among those interviewed, and some of the AIP oral-history projects, such as the International

Project in the History of Solid State Physics, have direct relevance to computer history.

The Smithsonian Institution holds a great many interviews on the history of computing. Most important are the 200 or so interviews of the AFIPS-Smithsonian Computer History Project, conducted in 1969 and 1970; Howard Aiken, John Atanasoff, Jay Forrester, Grace Hopper, An Wang, and Konrad Zuse are among the interviewees.

At the Massachusetts Institute of Technology are transcripts of oral-history interviews with people such as Robert Everett, Jay Forrester, Harold Hazen, and Alan Perlis who took part in Project Whirlwind and other important pioneering work at MIT.

A number of companies, including IBM and Hewlett-Packard, have conducted oral histories of their engineers and scientists; in some cases these have been made publicly available, in others special permission is required for access.

Computing Artifact Collections

Michael N. Geselowitz

As the extensive use of illustrations in this volume indicates, the artifact is taking on significance in the study of the history of computing. While the study of the artifact has been central to some Western social sciences (e.g., anthropology) since their origins in the 19th century, historians have been slow to embrace material culture studies outside of a museum context. This may be somewhat under-standable given that the written record, not the artifact, is the backbone of historical research. As I have pointed out elsewhere (1993), given that the artifact falls greatly within the social sphere known as technology, historians of technology have not been the leaders they should have been in this field, although Pocius (1997), among others, sees the situation as improving. In any event, the history of electrical and computing technologies, being a very recent discipline, has been able to build on earlier work in the history of technology to recognize the importance of the artifact to historical analysis.

The History of Electrical Technology Group of the Society for the History of Technology held its initial meeting in December 1971 to discuss the preservation of source materials related to electrical history, and specifically included artifacts in the category. This discussion led directly to the publication of a directory of artifact collections by Belfield in 1977, and interest among many of the participating historians of electrical technology continued to grow. In 1996 the Science Museum of London, the Smithsonian Institution, and the Deutsches Museum of Munich began what they hoped would be a series of joint conferences on

"Artifacts and the History of Technology." The first conference was broad in scope, but the second focused on one technology: electronics.

At that conference, whose proceedings are forthcoming, Frederik Nebeker summarized the reasons for incorporating the artifact into historical analysis: artifacts can provide motivation to learn about the past; artifacts can make book-acquired knowledge come to life; and artifacts can provide information not otherwise available. In this vein, I reported on the progress of the IEEE Center for the History of Electrical Engineering to update the 1977 directory and to expand it in two areas: geographical coverage; and the inclusion of computers, which are not surprisingly absent from the 20-year old publication. The following, drawn from that directory, is a basic summary of the sorts of collections that might be available and useful to the professional or amateur historian of computing looking for original artifacts.

There are literally hundreds of significant collections of electrical artifacts, both public and private. For the present purposes, I will restrict the discussion to collections which are formally designated as museums and are meant to be accessible to the public. Such a restriction leaves out private collections even if they are relatively accessible, if the owner has not established the collection as a museum. It also excludes public collections that are effectively inaccessible, even if they carry the label of "museum," such as those in the basements of some departments at public universities. Nevertheless, even this narrow definition leaves over 100 museums claiming to have computers among their holdings.

Not all of these collections are of equal value to the historian. The two most useful categories of museums for the history of computing are the small museum dedicated to the history of electronics or computing and the large museum of science, technology and industry, often a national concern. The former is a small, but I think growing category (which includes, for example, The Commercial Computing Museum in Kitchener, Ontario, the PC-Museum in Stenungsung, Sweden, the Historical Electronics Museum in Linthicum, Maryland, the American Computer Museum in Bozeman, Montana, and the Real World Computer Museum in Boothwyn, Pennsylvania). These are perhaps the best starting places for the computer historian looking for artifacts, since the staffs will be small but highly specialized.

Perhaps equally useful is the fact that many nations have a national museum of technology, and sometimes provinces or states, when large or wealthy enough, have their own such museum. These institutions often contain strong computer collections, depending on their own institutional history. Three that can be pointed to as outstanding are the three host institutions of the Artifact conference, the Science Museum, the National Air and Space Museum and the National Museum of American History of the Smithsonian Institution, and the Deutsches Museum, and, not exhaustively, other strong collections can be found at the National Museum of Science and Technology of Canada, and the Leonardo Da Vinci National Museum of Science and Technology in Milan. Such museums tend to be readily accessible, with relatively large and professional curatorial staffs that can be quite helpful. A researcher looking for original computing artifacts might be wise to start with these.

Then there are science/technology centers and, within those, specific museums of computing, where their main mission is to present current aspects of technology, primarily to children and usually in an interactive format. The historical holdings of these museums tend to be limited; often in their exhibitions that supply the historical context, replicas are used. However, some of the major computer museums do have significant collections (e.g., the Computer Museum in Boston, and The Computer Museum of Canada in Toronto). Such museums should be approached as a backup, or if one is specifically pointed toward them through prior research.

Finally, most of the museums with computer holdings turn out to be, in fact, museums of a regional focus and/or other intellectual focus that happen to have some computing equipment among their holdings because computing is tangential to their primary area of interest. The most obvious subcategory of this category is the military museum (e.g., The Royal Australian Artillery National Museum, in Manly, NSW, with its collection of calculating equipment used for targeting). Other subcategories include: regional museums in areas where computing played some role in the history (e.g., the York Castle Museum in England, which is dedicated to documenting local domestic life and economy and is currently building up its computer collection); the company museums of corporations involved in the computer industry (e.g., the Sharp Memorial Hall in Nara-ken, Japan) which may have computers mixed in with other products, but may lack key artifacts made by competitors; and museums of other technologies that involve computing but where computing is not the main focus (e.g., there are at least a score of extensive telephone museums worldwide, and many have several computing devices as part of their holdings). Such museums are mainly useful when a researcher is looking for a specific artifact or class of artifacts that he or she has reason to believe should be there because of the nature of the museum's holdings (e.g., an artillery computer in Manly; a Sony-made computer in Nara-ken).

Still, one can never be sure until the research is under way where appropriate artifacts of the history of computing and other electrical